THE MARXIAN

REVOLUTIONARY

IDEA

BY *Robert C. Tucker*

PHILOSOPHY AND MYTH IN KARL MARX
THE SOVIET POLITICAL MIND
THE MARXIAN REVOLUTIONARY IDEA

THE MARXIAN REVOLUTIONARY IDEA

◇◇◇◇◇◇◇◇◇◇◇◇◇◇◇◇◇◇◇◇◇◇◇◇◇◇◇◇◇◇◇◇◇◇◇

Robert C. Tucker

The Norton Library
W · W · NORTON & COMPANY · INC ·
NEW YORK

A publication of the Center of International Studies,
Princeton University

FIRST PUBLISHED IN THE NORTON LIBRARY 1970

The following copyright material is reproduced by permission: Chapters
1 and 2 from *Revolution: Nomos VIII* and *Justice: Nomos VI*, edited by
Carl J. Friedrich. (New York: Atherton Press, 1966 and 1963). Chapter 3
from *Marx and the Western World*, edited by Nicholas Lobkowicz.
(Notre Dame: University of Notre Dame Press, 1967). Chapter 5 from
"Paths of Communist Revolution 1917–1967," issued by the Princeton
Center of International Studies as a research memorandum. Chapter 6
from *The American Political Science Review* (June, 1967).

PRINTED IN THE UNITED STATES OF AMERICA

SBN 393 00539 9

3 4 5 6 7 8 9 0

FOR *Lisa*

Contents

Preface

This book deals with Marxism in two fundamental aspects. First, as theory—as a body of theory about man, history, society, and politics. Second, as ideology—as a radical social philosophy offering a vision of the good society and directions for its attainment. Hence it is not simply a study in the history of ideas. For Marxist radicalism has strongly impinged upon the life of society, and this interaction between Marxism and the real social world is one of the book's topics.

The first four chapters take up a series of basic themes in "classical Marxism," as the thought of Marx and Engels is called here. As a group they represent a kind of sequel to my earlier book, *Philosophy and Myth in Karl Marx*, which explored the roots of Marxism in foregoing German philosophy. Focusing particular attention upon Marx's youthful manuscripts, which expounded history as a story of man's alienation and its ultimate transcendence in communism, that book sought to show that the young Marx's philosophical communism remained at the core of the mature Marxian system. It argued that a fundamental line of continuity ran through Marxism from Marx's early philosophical writings to *Capital*, which, indeed, was simply the form in which he finally finished the book he set out to write in the 1844 manuscripts.

On the assumption that the controversy about the "young" and the "old" Marx has now about run its course, and that the underlying unity of Marx's thought has been established, I have undertaken in the present study to return to the major published writings of Marx and Engels from the new perspective that the investigation of the early Marx has given us. One chapter seeks to reformulate the classical Marxist theory of society of revolution. Another reexamines the ethical position of Marx and Engels, with particular reference to the idea of distributive justice. A third attempts a systematic exposition of their views on the state and politics. A fourth is devoted to the critical appraisal of classical Marxism as a theory of the modernization of societies. Since the social sciences in our time appear to be converging upon a theory of modernization as one of their central structures, this is an area in which Marx's persisting relevance is quite strong.

The discussion of Marxism as an ideology of revolutionary movements bulks large in the later chapters of the book. One of them takes up the problem of Marxism's appeal to the radical intelligentsia in underdeveloped countries, using nineteenth-century Russia as a principal illustration. Another looks into the various strategies by which communist movements have come to power over fifty years, and surveys the contributions of Lenin, Stalin, Khrushchev, Mao Tse-tung, and others to the Marxist theory of the revolutionary conquest of power. A third raises the question of what happens in radical movements of Marxist persuasion when, at length, they enter the phase of "deradicalization." Taking history as a laboratory, it analyzes the European social democratic movement of the late nineteenth century and Soviet communism of the mid-twentieth as examples of this phenomenon.

In our time, a resurgent radicalism among groups of student youth in Western society is groping for new ideological forms of expression. Existing Marxist ideologies are not likely to meet this need, nor will Marxism itself necessarily retain for much longer its century-old preeminence among radical social philosophies in the West. But whatever new radical amalgams may emerge, Marx's thought will in all probability remain a formative influence upon them and a powerful impulse within them. And to all who are concerned over the human situation, whatever their political outlook, Marx will continue to offer significant messages.

In my own personal credo concerning Marx, which I have undertaken to formulate anew in the concluding chapter of this volume, his enduring value lies especially in his "futurology." His vision of a matured humanity dwelling in a transformed world at the end of history remains one of the most relevant of human utopias.

Most of the chapters of this book have appeared earlier as essays, and I am grateful to the publishers for permission to publish them here. I am indebted to the Center of International Studies of Princeton University for free time during which the bulk of the book was written, and have enjoyed the opportunity to bring it to completion at the Institute for Advanced Study in Princeton. I wish to thank Stephen Cohen, Charles Elliott, Henry Bienen, Alistaire McAuley, and Daniel Tarschys for helpful comments and critical suggestions, and Mrs. Marilyn Hubbell for her expert assistance in typing the manuscript in final form.

R.C.T.

Princeton, New Jersey
1968

THE MARXIAN

REVOLUTIONARY

IDEA

Chapter One

THE MARXIAN REVOLUTIONARY IDEA

❖❖❖❖❖❖❖❖❖❖❖❖❖❖❖❖❖❖❖❖❖❖❖❖

In his parting word about Marx at Highgate Cemetery, Engels characterized his friend as "before all else a revolutionist." This was a true summation of Marx both as a man of action and as a thinker. For as a theorist Marx was before all else a theorist of revolution. The revolutionary idea was the keystone of his theoretical structure. Marxism, as he fashioned it with the assistance of Engels, was in its essence a theory and program of revolution.

Like many a powerful teaching that becomes the ideology of movements carried on in its name and dedicated to its realization, Marxism has not always reflected its original inspiration. It has tended at various times to lose its "revolutionary soul" (to borrow Lenin's phrase). This happened with the revisionist Marxism of Eduard Bernstein, who forsook even the revolutionary theory of Marx in favor of a doctrine of evolutionary socialism. It was reflected too, if less obviously, in the orthodox Marxism of Karl Kautsky, a leading theorist of the German Social Democratic party, whose fidelity to Marxist revolutionism in theory went along with an abandonment of it in practice. A similar if less pronounced discrepancy is becoming apparent in present-day Soviet Marxism. Its exponents rather resemble the German orthodox Marxists of a generation ago in their tendency to talk Marxist revolutionism while pursuing a relatively unrevolutionary policy. But all these instances of the decline of the revolutionary impulse in the Marxist movement belong to the story of what happened to Marxism after its founder's death. Our subject here is Marx's Marxism, and this was the world-view of a revolutionist.

It was so, moreover, from the beginning of his intellectual career. Marx's first independent act of theorizing, contained in notes to his doctoral dissertation of 1841, was an essay on the necessity of a complete revolutionary transformation of the world in the name of the "realization of philosophy," meaning the Hegelian philosophy of humanity's apotheosis in history. Marx was thus in some sense committed to the idea of world revolution prior to his conversion to the notions of socialism or communism, and he only accepted the latter a year or so later when he found a way of assimilating them into the philosophy of world revolution that he had evolved as a member of the school of Young Hegelian philosophers. Marxism was born of this fusion in an intellectual process recorded in Marx's *Economic and Philosophic Manuscripts of 1844*, whose publication in the present century presaged a new era in Marx scholarship in the West.

As a form of socialist doctrine, then, Marxism was inseparable from the idea of revolution. It conceived of socialism or communism (these two terms were always used by Marx and Engels more or less interchangeably) as a radically new state of the world, and of man in the world, which was to be achieved by revolutionary means. This, according to the *Communist Manifesto*, was what distinguished Marxism from the main currents of earlier socialist thought and most earlier socialist movements, which were essentially reformist rather than revolutionary.

The idea of revolution is present in nearly everything that Marx wrote. It is the theoretical axis of his early philosophical writings. It is the leitmotif of his great political pamphlets on the 1848 events, the *coup d'état* of Louis Bonaparte, and the Paris Commune. It informs almost all that he has to say on the strategy and tactics of the communist movement. It is a favorite subject in the voluminous correspondence that he carried on with Engels and others. And his major work, *Capital*, together with his other economic writings, is essentially a political economy of revolution, an inquiry into the conditions of capitalism's revolutionary self-destruction. In a basic sense, therefore, revolution was the master-theme of Marx's thought, and an exposition of the Marxian revolutionary idea in complete form would be nothing other than an exposition of Marxism itself as a theoretical system.

It follows that the Marxian revolutionary idea has as many dimensions of meaning as Marxism itself. Revolution for Marx is a social, an economic, a technological, a political, a legal, and an ideological phenomenon. It is even, in its way, a natural phenomenon, for it involves the appropriation of the man-produced world of material objects that Marx describes in his early writings as "anthropological nature" or the "nature produced by history." Furthermore, revolution means transformation of man himself. In Marx's words, "the whole of history is nothing but a continual transformation of human nature."[1] He especially looks to the future communist revolution as the source of a radical

1. *The Poverty of Philosophy* (Chicago: Charles H. Kerr, n.d.), p. 160.

transformation of man or "change of self," and here we touch upon the moral and religious dimensions of the Marxian revolutionary idea. Finally, revolution for Marx is an historical category. The whole of his theory of revolution is set in the frame of the materialist conception of history. His theory of society is a theory of society-in-history, and his theory of revolution is a theory of the transformations of society in history, a theory of history itself as a process of man's revolutionary evolution.

The Genesis of Marxism

Marx always maintained that his theory of history arose as a metamorphosis of Hegel's. The materialist conception of history was the Hegelian idealist conception turned "upside down" or "back upon its feet." The meaning of this enigmatic contention has become clear only in the light of the 1844 manuscripts, which show that Marxism was indeed born as a metamorphosis of Hegelianism.

Hegelianism treats world history as the self-realization of God or Spirit (*Geist*). Historicizing the creation of the world as conceived in the Judaeo-Christian theology, this philosophy pictures creation taking place in historical time as the process by which God becomes fully God *in* the world. Having at first externalized itself in the form of nature, Spirit, acting through humanity, creatively externalizes itself in a succession of historical civilizations or culture worlds, which it appropriates in thought stage by stage through the minds of the great philosophers down to Hegel. History is thus seen as a process of "production." God becomes fully God in the course of it by becoming aware of himself as such, for on Hegel's definition self-knowledge or self-consciousness belongs to the nature (or "concept") of God. For God to become aware of himself as such is, moreover, to become aware of himself as infinite being, or of all reality as Spirit, as subjective. Each historical episode of self-knowledge begins with Spirit confronted by a seemingly objective world of "otherness" outside and beyond it. This experience of being bounded by an object is portrayed by Hegel as an experience of finitude, which in turn is an experience of "alienation" (*Entfremdung*). The knowing mind, in other words, experiences the given objective world as alien and hostile in its otherness before recognizing it as Spirit in externalized form. Hence, knowing for Hegel is de-alienation whereby the given form of external reality produced by Spirit is stripped of its illusory strangeness and made "property of the ego."[2] The terminal point in the historical process of self-knowledge (which Hegel also describes as a progress of the consciousness of freedom through the overcoming of the fetters of finitude) is the stage of "absolute knowledge" when Spirit finally beholds the absolute totality of creation as Spirit and thus achieves complete self-realization in the knowledge of itself as Absolute Being. This self-knowledge, on Hegel's premises, is reached in Hegelianism—the scientific demonstration of the entire process of world history just summarized.

Marx originally formulated his materialist conception of history as a conscious act of *translation* of this Hegelian phenomenology of history into what he considered realistic or truly scientific terms. Following a lead given by Ludwig Feuerbach, he assumed that one had to draw a distinction between the manifest content of Hegelianism, which was mystical, and the latent or "esoteric" content, which was scientifically sound. What Hegel was esoterically talking about in his philosophy of history as the self-realization of God was the self-realization of humanity, the human histor-

2. *The Phenomenology of Mind*, trans. J. B. Baillie (London: George Allen & Unwin, 1931), p. 97.

ical process. Hegelianism was a philosopher's fantasy-picture of real human history. The task was to de-mystify it, which one could do by turning it upside down. That is, one had to switch the subject and predicate in the key propositions of Hegelian theory.

Thus man was not *Geist* in the flesh; rather, *Geist* was the thought-process in the head of real material man. History was not the process by which God becomes fully God in man; rather, Hegel's image of history as such a process was a mental representation of actual history as a process by which man becomes fully human. The world-creating activity going on in history was not thought-production, not something going on in God's mind; rather, the production of the world by Spirit was Hegel's mystified rendition of the real fact that the world is produced in a historical process of *material* production carried on by man in his economic life. Hence the true and scientific conception of history esoterically present in Hegelianism was a "materialist" one that views man as the universal creator and material production—the production of material objects—as the basic kind of human productive activity. By the same token, Spirit's experience of self-alienation in the presence of an alien and hostile world of its own creation was simply Hegel's mystified way of expressing the real fact that working man experiences alienation in the presence of a world of material objects that he himself has created in "alienated labor" in the service of another man—the capitalist—who appropriates the product as his private property. Appropriation (*Aneignung*) was not, therefore, something going on in the philosopher's mind; rather, the Hegelian notion of the cognitive appropriation of the world by Spirit was an inverted representation of the material appropriation of objects in history, the accumulation of capital. Further, the overcoming of alienation was not a process that could take place simply in thought. As the alienated world was a world of real material things and productive powers, the appropriation of it by the exploited and alienated producers, the proletarians, would have to take place in a real revolution —a communist revolution consisting in the worldwide seizure and socialization of private property. And finally, Hegel's picture of the ultimate stage of "absolute knowledge," when Spirit contemplates the whole world as Spirit in the beatific moment of complete self-awareness in freedom, was the philosopher's fantasy of ultimate communism, when man would achieve self-fulfillment in creative activity and aesthetic experience of the no longer alienated world surrounding him.

Such was Marxism, or the materialist conception of history, in its original presentation in Marx's 1844 manuscripts as an inverted Hegelianism. Much was refined and added in the subsequent development of the system by Marx and Engels. Yet this "original Marxism" was the matrix of the mature Marxist *Weltanschauung*. Even where a seeming break occurred, as in the abandonment of the category of "alienation" in the mature restatements of the theory beginning with Marx's in Part I of *The German Ideology*, we find an underlying continuity of thought; for the content of the idea of alienation lives on in the special meaning assigned in mature Marxism to the concept of "division of labor."

The fundamental ideas of original Marxism remained, explicitly or implicitly, the presuppositions of Marx's thought. Having defined history in the 1844 manuscripts as man's "act of becoming," he continued to see it as the process of self-development of the human species or society. For Marx history is the growth-process of humanity from the primitive beginnings to complete maturity and self-realization in future communism. Since man is conceived in this system as a creative being or producer in his essential nature, his developmental process is, as Marx had called it in his early manuscripts, a *Produktionsgeschichte* (history of production), with material production as the primary kind of productive activity. It proceeds through a series of epochs marked by the division of mankind into warring classes towards the postulated communist future. The transitions from epoch to epoch are revolutionary, for "revolutions are the locomotives of history."[3]

Marxism as Social Theory

Understandably, much of the literature of and about Marxism as a revolutionary theory has a political orientation. Marxists, beginning with Marx and Engels, have been deeply concerned with the politics of revolution, and very many students of Marxist thought have interested themselves in this too. It is perhaps a measure and in any event a symptom of this bias that Lenin's principal treatise on Marxist revolutionary theory, *The State and Revolution*, is almost wholly devoted to revolution as a political phenomenon. Now there is no doubt about the great importance of this aspect of the Marxian revolutionary idea. For Marx every revolutionary transition from one social epoch to the next involves a political revolution—the overthrow of the existing state and conquest of political power by the revolutionary class. But to Marx's way of thinking this is not the core of the revolutionary process. Here, indeed, we encounter a certain difference of emphasis between the Marxism of Marx and that of Lenin, for whom the political process of revolution was of supreme importance both theoretically and practically. Without ever slighting the significance of the political dimension, Marx, on the other

3. Marx, *The Class Struggles in France 1848–1850* (New York: International Publishers, n.d.), p. 120.

hand, always saw *social* revolution as the fundamental revolutionary fact. In the analogy between revolution and the birth-process that recurs from time to time in his writings, the social revolution is the whole organic process by which a new society comes into being; the political revolution is merely a momentous incident occurring at the climax of the process. The principal question to be considered here, therefore, is what Marx meant by a social revolution.

In *The Social Revolution*, an influential little volume written in 1902, Kautsky answered this question in behalf of German orthodox Marxism by defining social revolution as "the conquest of political power by a previously subservient class and the transformation of the juridical and political superstructure of society, particularly in the property relations. . . ." As Kautsky himself pointed out, this was a "narrower" view than Marx's own as expressed in the well-known preface to the *Critique of Political Economy*.[4] It also suffered from superficiality. Although the supplanting of one ruling class by another is integral to social revolution as Marx conceives it, this formula fails to convey the substance of what he means by social revolution. To arrive at a more adequate formulation, we must first consider Marx's conception of society.

Marx the sociologist is inseparable from Marx the theorist of history. The view of society presented in his own mature writings and those of Engels is governed at every point by the basic premises of the materialist conception of history. Thus, Marx as a social theorist recognizes the existence of societies on a national scale but does not see in them the fundamental unit of society. For him the real social unit is the species, the human collectivity at a given stage of its historical growth-process. Each such stage constitutes a social epoch dominated by a particular "social formation."

4. Karl Kautsky, *The Social Revolution* (Chicago: Charles H. Kerr, 1913), pp. 6, 8–9, 27.

Any national society, such as the German, English, or French, is but a concrete expression of human society as a whole in the given epoch, although it may be a case that exhibits the general pattern of the existing or emerging social formation most clearly and in most mature development. Marx, for example, saw contemporary English society as the model and most advanced form of a universally emerging "bourgeois society" of the modern epoch. This bourgeois or capitalist social formation, now becoming dominant on a world scale, had been preceded in history by feudal, antique, and Asiatic social formations, each of which represented the dominant form of human society in its time. An important implication for Marx's theory of revolution is that he always sees a social revolution as universal in scope, as an event of world history. It may express itself here and there on a national scale, as in the French Revolution of 1789, but such a happening is only a partial and local manifestation of a world revolutionary process. For Marx all social revolutions are world revolutions.

The materialist conception of history underlies all other aspects of Marx's sociology. Man being essentially a producer and his history a "history of production," society, to Marx's way of thinking, is in essence a productive system and process. The constitutive fact of society is that human productive activity, especially the material production on which all else depends, is social in nature. In other words, production for Marx is a process going on not simply between man and nature but also between man and man. This "social process of production" is the core of the social process per se. Human society is fundamentally a society of production, a set of "social relations" that men enter in the activity of producing. In the familiar formulation from *The Critique of Political Economy*, the social relations of production constitute the "basis" (*Basis, Grundlage*) of society, over which rises an institutional superstructure and to which there corresponds a social mind expressed in various "ideological forms" (religion, philosophy, art, etc.).[5]

Since primitive times, according to Marx, the society of production has been a divided one. The social relations of production have been property relations between the immediate producers and those who, by virtue of their ownership and control of the means of production, have been able to appropriate the producers' surplus product as private property: slaves and slaveowners in ancient society, serfs and landowning nobles in feudal society, proletarians and capitalists in modern bourgeois society. Each one of these sets of social relations of production has been, in Marx's terminology, a specific form of the division of labor (*Teilung der Arbeit*) in production. This concept has a twofold meaning in Marxist thought. First, it refers to occupational specialization in all its forms beginning with the division between mental and physical labor and between town and country. But it also refers to what may be called the "social division of labor," meaning the division of society as a whole into a nonworking minority class of owners of the means of production and a nonowning majority class of workers. As already indicated, Marx holds that such a social division of labor has been the essential feature of human society so far in history. The prime expression of the division of labor is the class division of society. In Engels' words, "It is . . . the law of the division of labor which lies at the root of the division into classes."[6] Marx makes the same point more concretely when he writes:

In so far as millions of families live under economic conditions of existence that divide their mode of life,

5. Marx and Engels, *Selected Works* (Moscow: Foreign Languages Publishing House [Vol. I, 1958; Vol. II, 1951]), I, 363.

6. *Herr Eugen Dühring's Revolution in Science (Anti-Dühring)* (Moscow: Foreign Languages Publishing House, 1947), p. 418.

their interests, and their culture from those of other classes, and put them in hostile contrast to the latter, they form a class.[7]

The determination of the class structure of society by the nature of the social division of labor may be expressed in Marxist terms by saying that every society is characterized by its particular "mode of production" (*Produktionsweise*). Contrary to what one might suppose, this key concept of Marx's is primarily social rather than technological in content, although it has a technological element. The mode of production is not equated with the productive techniques or material "productive powers," which are included, rather, under the heading of "means of production" (*Produktionsmittels*). What Marx means by the mode of production is the prevailing mode of labor or productive activity as conditioned by the existing state of technology or means of production. Now productive activity, as already noted, is for Marx exclusively and essentially social activity. Accordingly, the mode of production is equivalent to the social relations of production viewed, as it were, dynamically or in motion, together with the conditioning state of technology. And inasmuch as the social relations of production have so far in history been successive forms of the division of labor in production, the various historical modes of production may be described as forms of productive activity within the division of labor. Production within the division of labor has thus been the *general* mode of production in history. In Engels' formulation, "The basic form of all former production is the division of labor, on the one hand within society as a whole, and on the other, within each separate productive establishment."[8]

7. *The Eighteenth Brumaire of Louis Bonaparte* (New York: International Publishers, n.d.), p. 109.
8. *Anti-Dühring*, p. 432.

The central thesis of Marxist sociology is that every society in history has been characterized and indeed shaped in all its manifold aspects by the nature of its particular mode of production as just defined. In ancient society the mode of production was slave labor, or productive activity performed within the social division of labor between master and slave. In feudal society it was serf labor, or productive activity performed within the social division of labor between nobleman and serf. And in modern bourgeois society it is wage labor, or productive activity carried on within the social division of labor between capitalist and proletarian. In every instance—runs the argument of Marx and Engels—the mode of productive activity has been the definitive fact of the social epoch, the determinant of the character of society in all of its superstructural expressions: political, legal, intellectual, religious, etc. To this way of thinking, every society fundamentally *is* its mode of production. Of wage labor, for example, Marx writes: "Without it there is no capital, no bourgeoisie, no bourgeois society."[9]

It follows that a social revolution in the Marxist definition is a change in the mode of production with consequent change of all subordinate elements of the social complex. The feudal revolution would be defined in these terms as the change from slave labor to serf labor resulting in the general transition to feudal society; the bourgeois revolution as the change from serf labor to wage labor resulting in the general transition to bourgeois society. Historically, argue Marx and Engels, these revolutions in the mode of production and therewith in society as a whole have been changes of the *specific form* of productive activity within the social division of labor. They have been revolutions within the general mode of production based upon the division of labor in society and the production process, i.e.,

9. *The Class Struggles in France*, p. 42.

upon the class division of society and occupational special-ization.

Turning to the technological aspect of the theory, Marx holds, as pointed out above, that every historical mode of production has been conditioned by the nature of the available means of production or state of technology. As he puts it in a vivid passage, "The windmill gives you society with the feudal lord; the steam-mill, society with the industrial capitalist."[10] According to this view, the rise of a new technology, a new set of material productive powers, will necessarily prove incompatible with the perpetuation of a mode of production associated with an older one. The rise of modern manufacturing techniques led to the bourgeois revolution against serf labor and feudal society and to the enthronement of wage labor as the mode of production. Marx further supposes that the transition from early capitalist manufacture to "machinofacture" in the Industrial Revolution has brought into existence a new set of productive powers—modern machine industry—that must and will prove incompatible with the perpetuation of wage labor as the prevailing mode of production, since the new powers of production cannot be fully developed under the system of wage labor. The destruction of wage labor, and with it of bourgeois society, in a proletarian and communist revolution is the predicted outcome. Reasoning in this way, Marx and Engels frequently define a social revolution as the resolution of a conflict or "contradiction" between the productive powers and the social relations of production, or as a "rebellion" of the former against the latter.

This "rebellion" is not understood in mechanistic terms. A social revolution originates in technological change but actually takes place, according to Marx, in a revolutionary social-political movement of producers as a class. It is not the material powers of production themselves, such as the

10. *The Poverty of Philosophy*, p. 119.

machines, that rebel against the mode of production; it is the men involved. This presents no problem of inconsistency for Marx, however, because he views working man as the supreme productive power. "Of all the instruments of production," he writes, "the greatest productive power is the revolutionary class itself."[11] It is this productive power whose uprising constitutes the actual revolutionary process. The revolt of the productive powers against the existing social relations of production finds its manifestation in class warfare in the economic arena, culminating in the political act of revolutionary overthrow of the state. If revolutions are the locomotives of history, class struggles are the locomotives of revolution.

The Springs of Revolution

What motivates a class of producers to rise against and revolutionize a mode of production and its social superstructure? Suffering caused by material want and poverty is one of the immediate driving forces of revolutionary action, especially with the modern proletariat. But in Marx's view, material satisfaction as such is never the actual aim of the revolutionary class in its struggle to overthrow and transform an established social formation. What is fundamentally at issue in the class struggle and in social revolution, as in history as a whole, is not the consumption interest but the production interest—this, however, defined in a special Marxist way.

It is man as frustrated producer rather than man as dissatisfied consumer who makes a revolution, and the need of man as producer is to freely develop and express his manifold powers of productive activity, his creative potentiali-

11. *Ibid.*, p. 190.

ties in material life. Under this heading Marx includes both the productive powers within men, and industry or the material productive forces employed by the human species in its productive interaction with nature. Thus in *Capital* he describes the material forces of production as "the productive organs of men in society" and compares them with "the organs of plants and animals as productive instruments utilized for the life purposes of these creatures."[12] His thesis is that the source of revolutionary energy in a class is the frustration of man in his capacity of producer, his inability to develop new powers of production to the full within the confines of an existing mode of production or socioeconomic order. The bourgeois revolution, for example, results from the inability of the rising capitalist class to develop the new productive powers inherent in manufacture within the cramping confines of feudal relationships. And Marx believes—wrongly as it turns out—that a proletarian revolution will be necessitated by the impossibility of fully developing the productive potentials of modern machine industry within the confines of wage labor as the mode of production. In each instance the effect of the revolution is to eliminate a set of social relations of production that has become, in Marx's Hegelian terminology, a "fetter" upon the evolving productive powers of the species, and thus to "emancipate" these powers. The goal of all social revolutions, according to Marx, is freedom, but freedom in a specifically Marxist sense: the liberation of human creativity.

The obstacle to freedom, the source of human bondage, and thus the evil in history, is the division of labor. This fundamental proposition of Marxist theory has several meanings, all closely interconnected. Not only does each successive historical form of the social division of labor between an owning and a producing class become an impedi-

12. *Capital*, trans. Eden and Cedar Paul (London: J. M. Dent & Sons, 1933), p. 392 n.

ment to the free development of emergent productive powers; the social division of labor is also a force for enslavement in that it subjects the producer class to the acquisitive urge of the owning class, the insensate greed for possession and power that Marx sees as the dominant motive force of historical development up to now. (We read in Engels: " . . . it is precisely the wicked passions of man—greed and the lust for power—which, since the emergence of class antagonisms, serve as levers of historical development . . .".[13]) Man's life in production is thereby transformed into a life of drudgery, of forced or "alienated labor," as Marx called it in his manuscripts of 1844, and as he always continued to view it. Above all is this true in modern society, where the worker, although legally free to seek employment wherever he will, is bound down to wage labor, which Marx calls "wage slavery" and describes, in *Capital* and other writings, as productive activity performed in servitude to the capitalist profit mania, the "werewolf hunger" for surplus value.[14]

Finally, every social division of labor is an enemy of human freedom, for Marx, insofar as it enforces occupational specialization as a way of life.

> For as soon as labor is distributed, each man has a particular, exclusive sphere of activity, which is forced upon him and from which he cannot escape. He is a hunter, a fisherman, a shepherd, or a critical critic, and must remain so if he does not want to lose his means of livelihood. . . .[15]

It is Marx's view, in other words, that a division of labor under which men are compelled by economic necessity to

13. *Ludwig Feuerbach and the End of Classical German Philosophy*, in Marx and Engels, *Selected Works*, II, 345–346.

14. *Capital*, p. 269.

15. Marx and Engels, *The German Ideology*, parts I and III, ed. R. Pascal (New York: International Publishers, 1947), p. 22.

devote themselves throughout life to one particular form of work activity, be it a specialized economic function, or a noneconomic calling such as a profession or governmental work, or even intellectual activity, is slavery. And this is by no means a view that Marx "outgrew" in the later development of his system. Thus he speaks, in the famous passage of "The Critique of the Gotha Program" on the higher phase of communist society, of the disappearance there of "the *enslaving* subordination of man to the division of labor."[16] Engels is just as explicit and even more concrete when he writes:

> not only the laborers, but also the classes directly or indirectly exploiting the laborers, are made subject, through the division of labor, to the tool of their function: the empty-minded bourgeois to his own capital and his own thirst for profits; the lawyer to his fossilized legal conceptions, which dominate him as a power independent of him; the "educated classes" in general to their manifold local limitations and one-sidedness, to their own physical and mental short-sightedness, to their stunted specialized education and the fact that they are chained for life to this specialized activity itself, even when this specialized activity is merely to do nothing.[17]

This is a theme that has not always been much emphasized or even noted in the literature on Marxism. An influential school of Soviet Marxists has even undertaken to expunge it from Marxism, denying that Marx was opposed to

---

16. Marx and Engels, *Selected Works*, II, 23. Italics added. The "Critique" was a set of marginal notes by Marx on a draft program for a united German workers' party.

17. *Anti-Dühring*, pp. 435–436.

occupational specialization as a way of life.[18] But this is to deny the undeniable. The proposition that occupational specialization is slavery and that it can and should be done away with is met constantly in the writings of Marx and Engels, including such major works of mature Marxism as *Capital* and *Anti-Dühring*, and it is of fundamental importance in Marxism as they understood it.

Underlying their condemnation of the division of labor is the philosophical anthropology inherited by Marxism from earlier German philosophy, Hegelianism in particular. Marx's *Mensch* resembles Hegel's *Geist* in that both are imbued with a need for totality of life-experience, for creative self-expression in all possible fields of activity. Thus Hegel speaks of Spirit as "manifesting, developing, and perfecting its powers in every direction which its manifold nature can follow," adding: "What powers it inherently possesses, we learn from the variety of products and formations which it originates."[19] It is the same with the human species in Marx's image of it. And in view of the fact noted earlier that Marx constructed the materialist conception of history on the premise that Hegel's *Geist* was a mystified representation of man in his history of production, it is not

18. It should be added that among Soviet Marxists there are also some defenders of the authentic views of Marx on this question. One is Academician S. G. Strumilin, who has accused the dominant school of Soviet Marxists of resorting to outright falsification of Marx's language in its effort to misrepresent the true Marxist position on the desirability and possibility of doing away with occupational specialization. This, he points out, was done by consciously mistranslating *Verteilung der Arbeit* as "division of labor" (the correct translation would be "distribution of labor") in a 1947 Russian translation of Marx's letter of July 11, 1868 to Ludwig Kugelmann. To prove that the mistranslation was deliberate, Strumilin mentions that the phrase was correctly translated in Vol. XXV of the Russian edition of the collected works of Marx and Engels, published in 1934 ("Razdelenie truda i vsestoronee razvitie lichnosti," *Voprosy filosofii*, No. 3 [1963] p. 39).

19. *The Philosophy of History*, trans. J. Sibree (New York: Dover Publications, 1956), p. 73.

at all surprising that the Marxist view of human nature shows this strain of Hegelian philosophical romanticism. Like Hegel's *Geist*, Marx's humanity develops and perfects its productive powers in every possible direction, and man as an individual shows this same tendency. A man's inherent bent—that is, his nature—is to become, as Marx puts it in *Capital*, "an individual with an all-round development (*total entwickelte Individuum*), one for whom various social functions are alternative modes of activity."[20] Consequently, the division of labor is unnatural and inhuman, an impediment to a human being's self-realization. A person who applies himself to one single life-activity is alienated from his real nature, hence a self-estranged man. "In the division of labor," writes Engels, "man is divided. All other physical and mental faculties are sacrificed to the development of one single activity."[21] Even the division between town and country, between urban and rural labor, is on this view "a subjection which makes one man into a restricted town-animal, the other into a restricted country-animal."[22] And to be restricted to a particular kind of life or occupation is to be unfree.

The enslavement and dehumanization of man under the division of labor is a dominant theme of *Capital* and the other writings of Marx and Engels on capitalism and the proletarian revolution. They morally condemn capitalism not for being unjust as a mode of distribution (indeed, they hold that it is the only just one in terms of the sole applicable criterion of judgment), but for being inhuman as a mode of production, an unnatural way for man to carry on his productive activity. What makes it so, they maintain, is above all the hideous extreme to which it develops the division of labor. The capitalist mode of production—wage

20. *Capital*, p. 527.
21. *Anti-Dühring*, p. 435.
22. *The German Ideology*, p. 44.

labor in the service of the drive for surplus value—is a system of division of labor within the division of labor. That is, within the social division of labor between capitalist and proletarian, which Marx calls the "despotism" or "dictatorship" of capital, the worker is subjected to an increasingly oppressive form of occupational specialization. He is reduced to a mere detail worker bound down to a single mindless operation endlessly repeated. As capitalism evolves from the stage of "simple cooperation" into that of manufacture, it brings "the lifelong annexation of the worker to a partial function," which "cuts at the very roots of the individual's life" and "transforms the worker into a cripple, a monster, by forcing him to develop some highly specialized dexterity at the cost of a world of productive impulses and faculties—much as in Argentina they slaughter a whole beast simply in order to get its hide or its tallow."[23]

Moreover, the inner dynamism or dialectic of capitalist production is such—according to Marx's argument—that the functions become increasingly subdivided, the specialization more and more minute, and hence the fragmentation of man more and more monstrous, as the employers, under relentless pressure of the competitive struggle, strive for greater and greater technical efficiency through mechanization of work processes. The total dehumanization of the worker comes about finally under modern "machinofacture," the descriptions of which in *Capital* resemble a "Modern Times" without the Chaplinesque anodyne of humor. Of this stage—which he treats as the stage in which capitalist production becomes wholly unendurable—Marx writes, for example, that here all the means for developing production

mutilate the worker into a fragment of a human being, degrade him to become a mere appurtenance of the

23. *Capital*, pp. 381, 384, 390.

machine, make his work such a torment that its essential meaning is destroyed; estrange from him the intellectual potentialities of the labor process in very proportion to the extent to which science is incorporated into it as an independent power. . . .[24]

Progress in technological terms thus spells regress in human terms, and man sinks to the nadir of wretchedness and self-estrangement in the production process at the very time in history when his productivity, technically speaking, reaches its peak and—providentially—brings with it the possibility of a thoroughly human way of life in production. The "slavery" and "labor torment" under the division of labor represent a major share of the ever-increasing misery of the proletarian masses that drives them at length, according to Marx's argument, to revolt against their mode of production.[25]

The human history of production is thus also a history of revolution. The growth-process of society is propelled by a series of revolutions that center in major changes in the mode of production as a social process. These changes have been the very substance of the social history of man. It is true that Marx speaks of an "epoch of social revolution" as something occurring when a form of society nears its end.[26] Yet in a way he believes that history has always up to now been a revolutionary process, that man has always been at least incipiently in revolt against his mode of production. This, after all, is the sense of the opening statement of the *Communist Manifesto* that the whole of recorded history is a history of class struggles. Why it should be so on Marx's premises has been made clear. Every mode of production in history has been a form of productive activity within the division of labor, and the division of labor is bondage. In

24. *Ibid.*, p. 713.
25. *Ibid.*
26. "Preface to *The Critique of Political Economy*," in Marx and Engels, *Selected Works*, I, 363.

Marx's mind, history is a succession of man's revolutionary breaks out of the prison-house of the division of labor for freedom in the life of production.

No sooner has a new mode of production within the division of labor been established by revolutionary means than it too starts to become a "fetter" upon the ever-developing productive powers of the species. Such is the revolutionary dialectic of the historical process as Marx expounds it. Just as men begin to die biologically as soon as they are born, so societies embark upon their own revolutionary dissolution virtually from the time of their revolutionary "birth pangs." So we shall look in vain in Marx for a sociology in the sense of a theory of how societies work. His is a sociology of revolution, a theory of the internal dysfunctioning of the several historical societies, leading to their disintegration and downfall. Thus *Capital*, which is Marx's principal treatise on society and revolution as well as his chief work of economic theory, treats of the revolutionary rise, development, and fall of bourgeois society. And the whole thrust of the book is toward the "knell" of the proletarian revolution that it tolls in conclusion.

The Revolution of Communism

The proletarian revolution is described in various places by Marx and Engels as the overthrow of the bourgeois state and establishment of a proletarian dictatorship, accompanied by the forcible seizure and socialization of private property in the means of production. But this is only the external manifestation, the "phenomenal form" of the communist revolution. Like all previous social revolutions, the revolution of communism is for Marx and Engels essentially a change in the mode of production. And like all past revolutions, again, it is both destructive in that it does away with an old mode of production and constructive in that it establishes a new one in its place.

This presentation of the socialist or communist revolution, and hence of socialism or communism itself, as turning principally upon production, stands in substantial contrast with the view of most socialists, both of that time and now, that socialism is mainly concerned with the distribution problem. Marx and Engels were well aware of this difference. They often called attention to it in emphatic and even polemical terms. They argued that changes in the mode of distribution, leading to the practice of distribution according to needs in the higher phase of communist society, would only be incidental byproducts of a change in the mode of production that would be the real substance of the revolution of communism. Marx, for example, attacks what he calls "vulgar socialism" for the "consideration and treatment of distribution as independent of the mode of production and hence the presentation of socialism as turning principally on distribution." He states in the same passage that "it was in general a mistake to make a fuss about so-called *distribution* and put the principal stress on it."[27] In the same vein Engels pours scorn on Eugen Dühring for basing his "socialitarian" program on the unacceptable proposition that "the capitalist mode of *production* is quite good, and can remain in existence, but the capitalist mode of *distribution* is evil." He comments in this connection on "how puerile Herr Dühring's notions are—that society can take possession of the means of production without revolutionizing from top to bottom the old method of production and in particular putting an end to the old division of labor."[28]

If the communist revolution resembles all past revolutions in that it primarily revolutionizes the old mode of pro-

27. "Critique of the Gotha Program," in Marx and Engels, *Selected Works*, II, 23–24.
28. *Anti-Dühring*, pp. 443, 445.

duction, it also, according to Marx and Engels, differs from all other revolutions in history; and this thesis on the uniqueness of the projected world communist revolution is of the greatest importance in Marxist thought. The argument is that what undergoes revolutionizing in the communist revolution is not simply a particular form of productive activity within the division of labor (in this case wage labor), but the division of labor as such. Instead of replacing one form of productive activity within the division of labor by another, as the bourgeois revolution replaced serf labor by wage labor, the communist revolution will pave the way for a radically new mode of production that altogether abolishes and transcends the division of labor and therewith "labor" itself in the sense in which mankind has always known it (i.e., in the sense of "alienated labor" in the terminology of the 1844 manuscripts). As the younger Marx formulated it,

> In all revolutions up to now the mode of activity always remained unscathed and it was only a question of a different distribution of this activity, a new distribution of labor to other persons, whilst the communist revolution is directed against the preceding *mode* of activity, does away with *labor*, and abolishes the rule of classes with the classes themselves. . . . [29]

Over twenty years later the older Marx was saying the same thing when he wrote in *Capital* that the "revolutionary ferments" in modern capitalist society have as their aim "the abolition of the old division of labor."[30]

By the abolition of the old division of labor he and Engels mean, first, the abolition of the class division of society into owners of the means of production and nonowning workers. This will spell the abolition of wage labor after an

29. *The German Ideology*, p. 69.
30. *Capital*, p. 527.

interim during which old habits of working for a remuneration, and also the lack of full material abundance, will enforce a continuation of wage labor in a noncapitalist form, performed for social needs rather than in the service of the drive for profit. The disappearance of the latter as the motive force of production will make possible the withering away of the division of labor in all its subordinate forms— the division between mental and physical labor, between urban and rural labor, between different trades and professions, and between different functions in each. For as soon as man is no longer compelled by the imperatives of greed and the need to engage in some one form of productive activity all his life, he will give rein to the natural human tendency (as Marx sees it) to become a universal man —"to do one thing today and another tomorrow, to hunt in the morning, fish in the afternoon, rear cattle in the evening, criticize after dinner, just as I have a mind, without ever becoming hunter, fisherman, shepherd or critic."[31] Within the factory the detail worker, annexed for life to a particular specialized function, will give way to the "individual of all-round development" for whom various functions in production are possible. Marx based this expectation, which may have been prophetic, upon the view that in modern industry, where machines themselves do highly specialized work, the technical foundation is established for liberating men from narrow specialization. "Since the integral movement of the factory does not proceed from the worker but from the machine," he reasoned in *Capital*, "there can be a continuous change of personnel without any interruption of the labor process."[32] Machine industry without the division of labor would thus be based upon rotation of jobs among highly trained and versatile machine-operators, whose work would become a form of free productive ac-

31. *The German Ideology*, p. 22.
32. *Capital*, p. 449.

tivity owing to the constant variation and to the "almost artistic nature of their occupation."[33]

Since Marx and Engels believe that every form of society fundamentally *is* its mode of production, most of what they have to say about the future communist society (in its "higher phase") is naturally concerned with the anticipated new mode of productive activity. But the latter, as we see, is not analyzed in economic terms. This omission of an economics of communism from the theory of Marx and Engels is entirely logical considering that part of what they mean by communism is *the end of economics*. They assume that with the emancipation of the immensely potent productive forces inherent in modern machine industry from the "fetters" of capitalist wage labor, there will very soon be created a material abundance so great as to satisfy all proper human needs. At this point, which is the entry-point into the "higher phase," the historic scarcity of goods and resources ceases and therewith the need for economics as a theory and practice of allocation of scarce goods and resources. "And at this point," writes Engels, "man in a certain sense separates finally from the animal world, leaves the conditions of animal existence behind him, and enters conditions which are really human. . . . It is humanity's leap from the realm of necessity into the realm of freedom."[34] For Marx and Engels this "leap" is a take-off not into affluence as such but into the authentically human higher form of existence that man's creative and artistic nature, as they see it, naturally tends toward and for which material well-being is no more than a precondition. The end of economics means the beginning of aesthetics as the keynote of the life of productive activity.[35]

33. *Ibid.*, p. 405.
34. *Anti-Dühring*, pp. 420–421.
35. For a fuller exposition of this theme in Marxist thought, see R. Tucker, *Philosophy and Myth in Karl Marx* (Cambridge: Cambridge University Press, 1961), ch. 13.

In Marxist theory the communist revolution is the supreme revolution of freedom since it does away not simply
with this or that specific form of the division of labor but
with all forms, and so with bondage as such. By the same
token, this is the last revolution. With production no longer
based upon a division of labor in society, there will be no
kind of social relations of production that could become a
fetter upon the productive powers and thereby precipitate
a further revolutionary upheaval. Accordingly, the communist revolution will bring to an end the historical growth-
process of humanity—the "prehistory of human society,"
as Marx called it in a well-known passage.[36] It will mark
the maturation of the species, the time when man finally
becomes fully human. In his early manuscripts Marx used
the terms "humanism" and "transcendence of human self-
alienation" to express this idea. Later the German philosophical terminology was abandoned, but the idea was not.
The communist revolution continued to be conceived as a
revolution of human self-realization.

The self-realization is understood by Marx in both collective and individual terms. On the one hand, it means the
completion of the whole historical process of self-development of the species, the becoming of human society. At this
point "socialized humanity" (*vergesellschaftete Mensch-
heit*) emerges out of what had been, all through recorded
history, a self-divided and inwardly warring human collectivity.[37] The communist revolution, an act of appropriation
by the vast majority of the totality of material means of
production, is the means by which this final transformation
is supposed to take place. The reasoning turns on Marx's
view, mentioned earlier, that industry, the total complex of
material instruments or powers of production, represents
the "productive organs of men in society." Seen in this per-

36. "Preface to *The Critique of Political Economy*," *op. cit.*, p. 364.
37. Marx, "Theses on Feuerbach," in *The German Ideology*, p. 199.

spective, the communist revolution is the act by which man in the mass reappropriates his own organs of productive activity, of which he has been dispossessed in history owing to the division of labor in its various forms. By this collective act—runs Marx's argument—the individuals of whom the mass is composed regain their creative potentialities: "The appropriation of a totality of instruments of production is, for this very reason, the development of a totality of capacities in the individuals themselves."[38] This is the basis on which Marx advances the thesis that the change of material circumstances brought about by revolutionary *praxis* coincides with "change of self."[39]

It follows that man must realize himself on the scale of the species before he can do so as an individual, that there is no self-realization without social revolution. Before the communist revolution, no one can be truly human; afterwards, all can and will become so. Then and then only will free creativity become the characteristic human mode of production, will labor become "not only a means of life but life's prime want."[40] Then only will the human society of production become one in which

productive labor, instead of being a means to the subjection of men, will become a means to their emancipation, by giving each individual the opportunity to develop and exercise all his faculties, physical and mental, in all directions; in which, therefore, productive labor will become a pleasure instead of a burden.[41]

Liberated from the acquisitive urge that has always in the past motivated the production process, and from the slavery of specialization that this has engendered, men will finally

38. *The German Ideology*, p. 66.
39. "Theses on Feuerbach," *op. cit.*, p. 198.
40. Marx, "Critique of the Gotha Program," *op. cit.*, p. 23.
41. *Anti-Dühring*, p. 438.

become freely creative individuals, accomplished in a multitude of life-activities, who produce without being driven to it by the forces of need and greed and who arrange their world according to the laws of beauty.

That the Marxian revolutionary idea has a moral meaning is clear enough. But this dimension would, it seems, be more accurately described as religious than as ethical in nature. Moral teachers desire man to be virtuous according to one or another understanding of virtue; religious ones—Marx among them—want him to be redeemed. In this connection it must be said that there is a close relation between revolution and religion. Though the founders of revolutionary movements need not be men of religion, the founders of religions tend in their way to be revolutionaries. They envisage for man a goal of supreme worth that involves his total self-transformation, the revolutionizing of himself as it were, and they give him directions concerning the way to the goal. Marx does the same, and on this account may be characterized as a revolutionist of religious formation. The goal had variously been called the Kingdom of God, Paradise, Nirvana, Satori, Salvation; he called it Communism. When he wrote in his eleventh thesis that the point was to change the world, the message was that changing the world outside of man, by revolutionary *praxis*, was the way to change man himself, totally. There is little question as to the religious quality of Marx's vision of the goal. The question that one could raise, in an examination of the religious aspect of his thought, is whether he offered valid directions as to the way.

Chapter Two

MARX AND

DISTRIBUTIVE

JUSTICE

◇◇◇◇◇◇◇◇◇◇◇◇◇◇◇◇◇◇◇◇◇◇◇◇◇

At the turn of the century it was a widely accepted view that Marxism, in distinction from most other socialist doctrines, was ethically empty. Such authorities of that time as Kautsky, Sombart, Croce, and Lenin were in agreement on this point. As they saw it, the various non-Marxian schools of socialist thought could be called "ethical socialism" since they tended to predicate socialism on the moral "ought." Marxism, on the other hand, ran in terms of causal relations. It had succeeded in showing the proletarian revolution and socialism to be the inevitable outcome of the developmental process or inner dialectic of modern capitalist society. Alone among modern socialist doctrines, therefore, it was "beyond ethics."

Granted that Marx was not a moral philosopher in the conventional sense and that his system was not an inquiry into the nature of the supreme good, still this line of argument no longer carries conviction. Marx and Engels did, of course, claim to have demonstrated that socialism was inevitable; and were critical, even scornful, of socialists who based the theory of socialism upon a moral imperative. Yet this is no real proof of the ethical emptiness of Marxism. For a theory of history—and Marxism is basically that— may have a moral theme or content without its being presented on ethical grounds, and it may on this account view the historically inevitable as also morally desirable. The Marxist theory is unquestionably a case in point. From its standpoint the existing order is not only doomed by history but deserves to die, and the coming proletarian revolution not only must, but ought to, take place. Marx vividly expressed this idea in a speech in London in 1856. Referring to the revolutionary upheaval that he thought impending, he went on:

> To revenge the misdeeds of the ruling class, there existed in the Middle Ages, in Germany, a secret tribunal, called the *Vehmgericht*. If a red cross was seen marked on a house, people knew that its owner was doomed by the *Vehm*. All the houses of Europe are now marked with the mysterious red cross. History is the judge—its executioner, the proletarian.[1]

Marx here visualized the future revolution as an act of retributive justice against a civilization so criminal in character that it deserved nothing less than capital punishment. The symbolism is moralistic through and through. It expresses the judgment embedded in Marxism that there *ought* to be a world revolution. And though the passage stands out because of its striking imagery, it is otherwise typical of many to be found scattered through the later writings.

In some deep sense Marx was a moralist—a thinker whose thinking is decisively governed by a concern with values

1. Marx and Engels, *Selected Works*, I, p. 360.

of good and evil. A moral theme somehow pervades his whole system of thought. This, at any rate, is a view that seems to have gained, or to be gaining, acceptance among Western students of Marxism. The problem is to determine the nature of this moral theme. Granted that Marxism morally affirms the historically inevitable, on what ground does it do so? Why, in Marx's view, ought there to be a world revolution? What is the basis of his value judgment to the effect that the present order is evil and that the future communist order will be good? These are various formulations of one and the same basic question of the moral interpretation of Marxism.

One of the suggested solutions is the proposition that distributive justice was the value. According to this view, the Marxist condemnation of capitalist civilization expressed, at bottom, a protest against the injustice inherent in capitalism, and Marxism morally affirms the proletarian revolution because it will inaugurate a reign of justice in human society. Such is the interpretation of Marx and Marxism implied in the following statement by Harold J. Laski: "At bottom, the main passion by which he was moved was the passion for justice."[2] Laski was echoed by A. D. Lindsay, who said of Marx: "His fundamental passion is a passion for justice."[3] Another English interpreter of Marxism, E. H. Carr, has suggested that justice is the moral theme of Marx's principal work: "In *Capital*, published twenty years after the *Communist Manifesto*, Marx demonstrated for the first time that the victory of the proletariat would be the victory not only of brute force, but of abstract justice."[4] A similar interpretation is suggested by Sidney Hook, who writes: "The ethics of Marx did not merely express a demand for

2. *Karl Marx* (New York: League for Industrial Democracy, 1933), p. 46.

3. *Karl Marx's Capital: An Introductory Essay* (London: Geoffrey Cumberlege, 1947), p. 114.

4. *Karl Marx: A Study in Fanaticism* (London: J. M. Dent & Sons, 1934), p. 83.

social justice but a specific *kind* of justice dependent upon the objective possibilities created by capitalism."[5] These are representative expressions of the point of view that takes the idea—or one of the ideas—of justice to be the moral key to Marxism.

There is no denying that much of what Marx and Engels wrote confers at least a superficial plausibility on such an interpretation. "Hitherto, every form of society has been based on the antagonism of oppressing and oppressed classes" runs the familiar statement of the *Communist Manifesto*. The drama of class struggle is a drama of oppression and resistance to oppression, and what if not injustice might lie at the core of this oppression? Does not the *Manifesto*, moreover, say that two of the first acts of the proletarian dictatorship should be the institution of a "heavy progressive or graduated income tax" and the "abolition of all right of inheritance"? Marx and Engels depict the capitalist society that they abhor as the scene of a great and growing inequality of wealth, where untold riches accumulate in the hands of a small and dwindling class of avaricious capitalist magnates while the masses of working people sink deeper and deeper into a black pit of poverty. Do they not, then, condemn capitalist society *because* of its inequalities? And finally, what is the capitalist "exploitation" of labor that Marxism talks about if it is not a relation in which the worker is robbed of what rightfully belongs to him? In all these ways Marxism invites a moral interpretation that sees distributive justice as its central issue.

On closer analysis, however, the writings of Marx and Engels not only fail to sustain such an interpretation, but also furnish conclusive evidence that it is untenable. The fundamental passion of the founders of Marxism was not a passion for justice. Their condemnation of capitalism was

5. *From Hegel to Marx: Studies in the Intellectual Development of Karl Marx* (New York: The Humanities Press, 1950), p. 53.

not predicated upon a protest against injustice, and they did not envisage the future communist society as a kingdom of justice. In general, they were opposed to the notion that socialism or communism turns principally on the matter of distribution. This is not to say that they were indifferent to working-class poverty and the great inequality of wealth. Nor is it to deny that very many later followers of Marxism have seen in their teaching a gospel of social justice and have been attracted to it for this very reason. Marxism has meant many things to many Marxists, just as have other millennial movements to their followers. The point is simply that the common image of Marx as a prophet of social justice is a false one and that those who have seen distributive justice as the main moral issue of his Marxism have been mistaken. In what follows I shall present the evidence for this thesis under three headings: direct testimony from Marx and Engels bearing on the question, their analysis of capitalist exploitation of labor, and their picture of the post-revolutionary society.

The Polemic Against the Idea of Justice

Originating in the first third of the nineteenth century in the teachings of Saint-Simon and Fourier in France and Robert Owen in England, modern European socialism displayed from the start a distributive orientation, a concern with the problem of distribution in society. This did not necessarily mean that the principle of distributive justice was uppermost in the thinking of socialists. For Saint-Simon and many later socialists, for example, the moral basis of socialism was not the ideal of justice but rather the ideal of human brotherhood or love. This was given classic expression in the socialist formula enunciated by Louis Blanc:

"From each according to his ability, to each according to his needs." This was not a formula for distributive justice or equity, since the needs of individuals may be in inverse proportion to their abilities and to their contribution to society, and in any case they will normally differ from person to person. What the formula expresses, therefore, is an ethic of brotherhood.

Among some socialist thinkers of the nineteenth century, however, the distributive orientation was linked with an ethic of justice. Foremost among these was Marx's French contemporary, Pierre Joseph Proudhon. Taking issue with the Saint-Simonians and others who predicated their socialism upon an ideal of brotherhood, he argued that the slogan, "From each according to his ability, to each according to his needs," was proper for a family but not realizable as the operative principle of a larger society. For him the ethical starting point was the dignity of the individual. Not love of others but respect for their dignity as persons was the proper basis of morality. And the formula for morality was justice, defined as mutual respect for human dignity. The key concept was "mutuality" or "reciprocity." This philosophy, to which Proudhon gave the name "Mutualism," underlay his plan to reorganize society as a *fédération mutualiste* composed of occupational groups functioning on cooperative principles under a system of reciprocal service. "Mutuality, reciprocity exists," he wrote, "when all the workers in an industry, instead of working for an entrepreneur who pays them and keeps their products, work for one another and thus collaborate in the making of a common product whose profits they share amongst themselves."[6]

Proudhon laid the theoretical foundations for Mutualism in his first major work, *What is Property?* (1840), which enunciated the doctrine that "property is theft." By "prop-

6. Quoted in Martin Buber, *Paths in Utopia* (London: Routledge & Kegan Paul, 1949), pp. 29–30.

erty," it should be explained, Proudhon did not mean individual possession and use of goods, including producer goods; this he called simply "possession" and did not regard as theft. "Property" meant, quite specifically, the right of the possessor of producer goods to employ wage workers and draw profit from their labor. This profit, consisting of a portion of the proceeds of labor that rightfully belonged to the laborer himself, was "theft." Anticipating Marx, Proudhon also called the relationship just described one of "exploitation of man by man, or bondage."[7] In *What Is Property?* his prescription for the social problem was to preserve the right of possession while abolishing the right of property in the special sense just defined. This was the idea behind his later program for reconstituting society as a federation of autonomous producer cooperatives within which and among which the principle of reciprocity of service, i.e., exchange of services on the basis of reciprocal equality, would be realized.

Proudhonism proved an influential current in European socialist thought. Especially important was Proudhon's idea that the wage worker under capitalism was being robbed of something that rightfully belonged to him, or that profit was theft. The obvious programmatic implication for socialists was the demand that the worker receive the "undiminished proceeds of labor." This and other similar slogans, such as "a fair distribution of the proceeds of labor," became increasingly prominent as socialist movements in Europe associated themselves with trade unionism and practical working-class politics. In Germany the slogan of fair distribution was vigorously promoted by the influential socialist thinker and politician Ferdinand Lassalle and his followers. Their influence was reflected, for example, in the Gotha program, a program for a united German workers'

7. P. J. Proudhon, *What Is Property? An Inquiry into the Principles of Right and Government*, trans. Benjamin Tucker (London, 1902), p. 257.

party that was drafted in 1875 and is now best known through Marx's posthumously published critique in a set of marginal notes privately written for the edification of the party leaders. One of the draft program's clauses reads:

> The emanicipation of labor demands the promotion of the instruments of labor to the common property of society and the cooperative regulation of the total labor with a *fair distribution of the proceeds of labor*.[8]

Marx's attack on this clause forms an appropriate introduction to a review of his position on distributive justice. He was incensed at the very idea that the German workers' party should demand a "fair distribution of the proceeds of labor" as part of its program. "What is a 'fair distribution'?" he inquires acidly. Do not the bourgeoisie claim that the present mode of distribution is the only "fair" one, and are they not right in their own frame of reference? Nor can socialists agree among themselves as to the meaning of "fair distribution": "Have not also the socialist sectarians the most varied notions about 'fair' distribution?"[9] Going on in the same vein for several paragraphs, Marx finally breaks into a tirade. He declares that such slogans as "fair distribution," "equal right," and "undiminished proceeds of labor," which might have had some meaning at one time, have now become "obsolete verbal rubbish" which it would be a "crime" to force upon the party again. The German party's hard-won realistic outlook should not be perverted by "ideological nonsense about right and other trash so common among the democrats and French socialists."[10]

Though unusually violent in language, this denunciation of the distributive orientation was otherwise representative of the position that Marx and Engels had been upholding for decades in both their private correspondence and their

8. Marx and Engels, *Selected Works*, II, 19. Italics added.
9. *Ibid.*, p. 20.
10. *Ibid.*, p. 23.

published writings. They showed contempt for socialists who attempted to ground a critique of capitalist society in the principle of justice. "It is really very superstitious of the fellow that he should still believe in the 'idea of justice,' absolute justice," wrote Engels in a letter to Marx of December 2, 1861, commenting on a new book by Lassalle.[11] Marx, ridiculing Proudhon for applying an ideal of justice to economic relations, inquired:

> Do we really know anything more about the "usurer," when we say that his actions conflict with "eternal justice," with "eternal equity," with "eternal mutuality," and with other "eternal verities"—than the Fathers of the Church knew when they said that the actions of the usurer conflicted with the "eternal grace," with the "eternal faith," with the "everlasting will of God"?[12]

These statements accurately reflect the Marxist viewpoint as it emerges from the texts themselves. The writings of Marx and Engels over a period of fifty years contain a torrent of testimony that the principle of distributive justice is alien to the mental world of Marxism.

Much of this testimony is provided by the polemic that Marx and Engels carried on for many years against Proudhon and his concept of socialism, which they classified under the heading of "Bourgeois or Conservative Socialism" in the *Communist Manifesto*. It is true that *What Is Property?* played a momentous part in the mental evolution of Marx during the formative period of his system in the early 1840's and that he always professed admiration for this book. However, in 1847 he published *The Poverty of Philosophy*, in which he declared intellectual war on the whole approach to social and economic problems in "the equalitarian system of M. Proudhon." The war went on without letup.

---

11. Marx and Engels, *Selected Correspondence 1846–1895* (New York: International Publishers, 1942), p. 128.
12. *Capital*, pp. 59–60.

Twenty-five years later, Engels was still waging it in his anti-Proudhonian pamphlet *The Housing Question*, one of the themes of which was the fatuousness of Proudhon's ideal of "eternal justice" in a society of equal exchange among individual producers each receiving the full value of his labor. Rejecting the very idea of "eternal justice," Engels here states that justice is "but the ideologized, glorified expression of the existing economic relations, now from their conservative, and now from their revolutionary angle." For the Greeks and Romans, slavery was just; for the bourgeoisie of 1789, feudalism was unjust. It all depends on time, place, and socioeconomic circumstance. And, even if one were to grant that expressions like "right," "wrong," and "justice" are usable in everyday life in view of the simplicity of the relations discussed, they have no place in any scientific investigation of economic relations. To go on talking about the idea of justice in relation to economic matters, as Proudhon does, is to create the same hopeless confusion as would be created, for instance, in modern chemistry if the terminology of the phlogiston theory were to be retained. "The confusion becomes still worse if one, like Proudhon, believes in this social phlogiston, 'justice.' . . ."[13]

Is Capitalism Unjust?

Does Marx consider the capitalist system unjust and condemn it on this ground? To many it has seemed so, especially in view of the central part that the concept of exploitation plays in his system. Marxism defines capitalism as a way of production founded on the exploitation of wage

13. Engels, *The Housing Question*, in Marx and Engels, *Selected Works*, I, 624–625.

labor for the accumulation of capital. "Exploitation" is a term that carries a conventional connotation of injustice. One party, the exploiter, receives more than is rightfully due him, and the other, the exploited, receives less. This, as noted above, was the position taken by Proudhon, for whom the exploitation of wage labor for profit meant theft or legalized robbery whereby the working man was deprived of part of the proceeds of his labor. It seems plausible to assume that Marx, who developed his own position in part under the influence of Proudhon's *What Is Property?*, understood "exploitation" in the same or a very similar way. But examination of the Marxist writings show this to be a false assumption.

In his specific analysis of capitalist society, Marx formulated the theory of exploitation more concretely as a theory of surplus value. He started here from the postulate of classical political economy that the exchange value of any commodity depends upon the amount of labor, or labor time, incorporated in it, labor being taken by Marx as the sole agent creative of exchange value. He then went on to argue that labor power—which itself becomes a commodity under capitalism—has the peculiar attribute of creating more new exchange value in a day's use than it itself, economically speaking, is worth. What it is worth—its own exchange value as a commodity—is equal to the amount of labor incorporated in it, i.e., the amount of labor required to produce enough means of subsistence to maintain the worker in a fit state to work and to reproduce his kind. Briefly, the value of the worker's labor power for a day, as determined by the general law of value in capitalist society, is a subsistence wage. However, in a full day's work for the capitalist, the labor power so purchased creates an amount of new exchange value greater than this. The discrepancy, greater or less depending on the length of the working day, is called by Marx "surplus value." He depicts capitalism as a system of exploitation of labor power for the amassing of surplus value ad infinitum. This exploitative relation of capital to labor is said to constitute the very essence of the capitalist mode of production, and the proletarian revolution is seen as having the mission of abolishing exploitation forever. As Engels expressed it, "This exploitation is the basic evil which the social revolution wants to abolish by abolishing the capitalist mode of production."[14]

The question at issue here is whether a concern for justice underlies this value judgment. The objection to the affirmative view is that it flies in the face of the most emphatic and unequivocal assertions by both Marx and Engels that their condemnation of capitalist exploitation has nothing whatever to do with justice and injustice. They explain in this connection that the exploitation of wage labor for the accumulation of capital cannot be described as unjust. On the contrary, it is perfectly just or equitable in accordance with the only applicable norms of justice—those operative in the existing mode of production and exchange. Since the subsistence wage represents the full value of the worker's labor power as a commodity, he is not being robbed or cheated or treated unjustly when he receives less than the full produce of his day's labor as recompense. The labor time during which he creates surplus value for the capitalist rightfully belongs to the capitalist as the purchaser of a day's labor power of the worker at full value. In Marx's own explicit statement in *Capital*:

> It is true that the daily maintenance of the labor power costs only half a day's labor, and that nevertheless the labor power can work for an entire working day, with the result that the value which its use creates during a working day is twice the value of a day's labor power.

14. *Ibid.*, p. 558.

So much the better for the purchaser, but it is nowise an injustice (*Unrecht*) to the seller.[15]

Having purchased the labor power for a day at full value, the capitalist, in other words, has every right to appropriate all the value that the exercise of the labor power for a day creates. This leaves open, of course, the issue of the exact length of the working day, and here, according to Marx, there is simply no determining what is right and just. The capitalist is merely exercising his right when he attempts to prolong the working day further, and the worker is exercising his when he resists: "Here we encounter an antinomy in which right conflicts with right, both of these rights being hallowed by the law of exchange of commodities. When two rights come into conflict, force decides the issue."[16]

The Marxist conclusion is that the wages of the worker under capitalism are all that he has any right to and that the surplus value appropriated by the capitalist is no more than he has a right to. The capitalist mode of distribution, as determined by the law of exchange of commodities in capitalist society, is entirely fair, just, and equitable in capitalist terms. But is there no standard of justice superior to the one implicit in the capitalist "law of exchange of commodities," no general criterion of right by reference to which the capitalist exploitation of labor, although just enough on capitalist principles, might be pronounced unjust per se? The answer given by Marx and Engels is clearly and def-

---

15. *Capital*, p. 188. The same point was later made by Engels in practically the same words: "The circumstance that the value which the use of it (i.e., the labor power) during one day creates is double its own value for a day is a piece of especially good luck for the buyer, but on the basis of the laws of exchange of commodities by no means an injustice to the seller" (*Anti-Dühring*, p. 305).

16. *Capital*, pp. 234–235.

initely negative. "Right," according to Marx, "can never be higher than the economic structure of society and its cultural development thereby determined."[17] "Social justice or injustice," according to Engels, "is decided by one science alone—the science which deals with the material facts of production and exchange, the science of political economy."[18] In short, the only applicable norm of what is right and just is the one inherent in the existing economic system. Each mode of production has its own mode of distribution and its own form of equity, and it is meaningless to pass judgment on it from some other point of view. Thus, capitalism for Marx and Engels is evil but not inequitable. They do not accept Proudhon's interpretation of exploitation. They do not admit that profit derived from wage labor under the capitalist system is "theft." We may therefore conclude that the Marxist condemnation of capitalism is not predicated upon a belief that its mode of distribution is unjust.

Justice and the Post-Revolutionary Future

Turning now to the third area of evidence—the Marxist view of the post-revolutionary future—the question is whether Marx and Engels show a distributive orientation in their thinking about socialism or communism and, more concretely, whether they envisage the future communist society as a realm of distributive justice. Although they left no detailed prospectus of communism as a social system, material pertinent to this question is to be found here and there in their writings. The best-known statement is Marx's

17. "Critique of the Gotha Program," in Marx and Engels, *Selected Works*, II, 23.
18. Marx and Engels, *Kleine Ökonomische Schriften* (Berlin: Dietz Verlag, 1955), p. 412.

in the *Critique of the Gotha Program,* where he draws the distinction between the two phases of communist society—the short transitional phase (later called "socialism" in the Marxist literature) and the "higher phase" beyond it.

It is noteworthy that this *locus classicus* of the Marxist view of communism occurs in the context of Marx's angry attack, examined above, on the concept of "fair distribution." Having asserted that capitalist distribution is the only fair distribution under the capitalist mode of production and that the "socialist sectarians" are anyhow unable to say what a "fair distribution" would mean to them, Marx went on to argue that in principle "bourgeois right" will still prevail during the first phase of communist society. Though production for profit will presumably have stopped, exchange will still be based on commodity equivalents: so much labor time in one form (labor) will be exchanged for an equal amount of labor time in another form (consumption goods). Furthermore, said Marx, the application of this essentially bourgeois standard of equality will make the first phase of communist society a realm of *in*equality, since individuals are unequal in native endowment and in needs. Thus individuals will receive equal recompense for periods of labor in which one works harder and more efficiently than another, and individuals with equal pay will be in unequal circumstances owing to differences of family status, and so on.[19]

So much for the lower phase; what about the "higher phase" or true communist society? Here at last, according to Marx, it will become possible to transcend the "narrow

19. "Critique of the Gotha Program," *loc. cit.* Engels made the same point in a letter to Bebel in 1875: "The notion of socialist society as the realm of equality is a superficial French idea resting upon the old 'liberty, equality, fraternity'—an idea which was justified as a *stage of development* in its own time and place but which, like all the superficial ideas of the earlier socialist schools, should now be overcome, for they only produce confusion in people's heads and more precise forms of description have been found" (*Selected Correspondence,* p. 337).

horizon of bourgeois right." People will receive according to their needs. At this point Marx quotes, for the first and only time in his writings, the old French socialist formula, "From each according to his ability, to each according to his needs." As pointed out earlier, this is not a formula for justice. Nevertheless, it does connect the idea of communism with a principle of distribution. It injects a distributive theme into the discussion of communism. All the more significant, therefore, is the fact that, having done this, Marx immediately returns with great vehemence to the antidistributive main theme of his argument. Dismissing the notions of equal right and fair distribution as obsolete verbal rubbish which it would be an outright crime to foist upon the German workers' party, he goes on, "Quite apart from the analysis so far given, it was in general a mistake to make a fuss about so-called *distribution* and put the principal stress on it." It was characteristic of "vulgar socialism" to give a presentation of socialism as turning principally on distribution; "why retrogress again?"[20] From all this it should be abundantly clear that Marx does not envisage communism as a realm of distributive justice and that, although he does refer on this one occasion to the well-known formula on distribution according to needs, communism, in his conception of it, does not turn principally on distribution.

The Underlying Issue

The issue implicit in Marx's repudiation of the distributive approach goes to the philosophical core of Marxism. His contention that socialism or communism should not be conceived in fundamentally distributive terms concealed and, in a negative way, revealed his own positive conviction, rooted in the basic thought-pattern of Marxism, that social-

20. "Critique of the Gotha Program," *op. cit.*, pp. 23–24.

ism or communism should be conceived primarily in terms of *production*. If a distributive orientation was characteristic of most socialist doctrines in the nineteenth century, a production orientation was characteristic of Marx's. By this I mean that the central concern of Marxist theory, morally as well as intellectually, is with the mode of production, with man's activities as a producer, and with the conditions under which he carries on these activities. This production orientation, as has been shown in the previous chapter, belongs to Marx's philosophical inheritance as a thinker of Hegelian formation.

Communism itself was envisaged in terms of a fundamental transformation of the mode of production. Classical Marxism holds that the communist revolution, by destroying the division of labor in society into capitalists and workers, will eliminate wage labor itself as a mode of production. In other words, it will eliminate production for profit, for accumulation of capital, as a way of carrying on the human life of production, although, as noted above, Marx foresees that the wage system in a new form will continue briefly in the transitional phase of proletarian dictatorship. However, the ensuing "higher phase" of communist society is to be marked by the total "emancipation of labor" from all historic forms of division of labor and from the bondage, torment, and misery involved in each. This is Marx's conception of communism. He alludes to it in the very passage of the *Critique of the Gotha Program* that contains the well-known reference to distribution according to needs. In the "higher phase," he says, the "enslaving subordination of the individual to the division of labor" will have ended, and labor will have become "not only a means of life but life's prime want."[21] This was the vital part of the passage for Marx.

All this lies in the background of Marx's opposition to the distributive orientation and the idea of justice. Regarding

21. *Ibid.*, p. 23.

the problem from the point of view that has just been briefly summarized, he could not help but consider it crass, vulgar, superficial and simply wrongheaded for a socialist to put the emphasis on the distributive aspect or espouse justice as a social ideal. For Marx the basic and burning issue was the life of production. What made capitalism evil and condemned it to death before the *Vehmgericht* of history was the antihuman character of wage labor itself as a way of leading the life of production. The crime for which the existing order deserved capital punishment by its executioner the proletarian was the dehumanization of man under a division of labor that transformed his productive activity into "labor torment," that reduced him in the factory to a mere fragment of a man bound to some minute, mindless operation endlessly repeated. And, by the same token, what made communism appear so desirable to Marx was the revolution in the mode of production and therewith in the state of man the producer, that, as he saw it, would inevitably result from the coming proletarian upheaval and abolition of private property on a world scale. Freed from his age-old imprisonment in the division of labor, which had reached its most intolerable extreme in the capitalist stage of history, man could and would finally become fully human. He would achieve self-fulfillment in his essential role as a producing animal. The new mode of production, marking the maturity of the race after the long painful development in history, would be akin to art. Naturally men would now have enough to eat and generally be released from material worries. But this was not the essential thing, for the main content of man's life was producing and not consuming.

Given this notion that the basic evil of the existing order resided in the mode of production, it naturally seemed senseless or worse to Marx for socialists to complain about inequities of distribution. First, the low rate of pay, the great disparity of reward between capitalist and worker, was but one of many symptoms of the situation that needed correcting. As such, however, it was inherent in a system of production that subordinated everything to the one overriding aim of accumulation of capital out of surplus value; hence nothing much could be done about it on this side of world revolution. Further, even if some small improvements in pay and working conditions—such as the ten-hour day in England—could be wrested from the capitalists, these represented palliatives rather than a real solution or the beginning of one. No mere rectification on the distributive side could make the evil mode of production tolerable. Moreover, to suggest the contrary, as was done by those socialists who called for "fair distribution of the proceeds of labor," was to run the risk of disorienting the proletarians, of sidetracking their spontaneous revolutionary strivings and tendencies into the pathways of piecemeal reform within the present order. Such slogans were calculated to sow in the workers' minds the illusion that their problems could be resolved and their suffering alleviated without a fundamental revolutionizing of the mode of production. From Marx's point of view, therefore, the distributive orientation ultimately pointed the way to abandonment of the revolutionary goal. His fears on this score were, of course, well grounded, as was shown by the later evolution of social democracy in Europe.

The ground of Marx's aversion to the idea of justice is now not far to seek. The idea of justice connotes a rightful balance in a situation where two or more parties or principles are in conflict. It typically involves an adjustment or settlement based on a delimitation of mutual claims. Now for socialists to raise the cry of justice with reference to economic relations in capitalist society was to imply that a rightful balance might be struck, or an adjustment reached, in the conflict between capital and labor. It was to suggest the possibility of a negotiated peace or, at any rate, armistice, in the warfare between capital and labor. This was anathema to Marx. As he saw it, there was no possibility of settling this conflict, no way of achieving a delimitation of mutual claims between these two antagonists. The civil war in modern society was a battle unto death. The only possible formula for peace was the total victory of labor and the total destruction of capital as a social force. To Marx's mind, therefore, socialists like Proudhon, who preached social justice, were misguided and dangerous men. They were misguided because they failed to see the irrelevance of the idea of justice to the social problem, the inconceivability of any adjustment of claims or settlement of the conflict in modern society short of a revolution of the mode of production. And they were dangerous because this inclined them to pursue (in the phraseology of a later age) a no-win policy in the class struggle instead of a policy of victory looking to the establishment of total peace in the classless society.

Marx's issue with Proudhon over the idea of justice may be seen, ultimately, as an issue over unity and conflict in human society. Proudhon was opposed in principle to a search for unity in society. He argued that contradiction, that is, conflict or antagonism, is the first law of the universe and that justice or mutuality is the principle of balance or equilibrium of antagonisms. Borrowing the Hegelian dialectical categories of thesis, antithesis, and synthesis, he defined justice as the reconciliation of opposing claims in a higher synthesis. This, for example, was his approach to economic problems in *The System of Economic Contradictions, or The Philosophy of Poverty*, to which Marx responded in 1847 with his scathing attack, *The Poverty of Philosophy*, and with repeated attacks in later years. And in these attacks Marx specifically assailed the dualistic or pluralistic idea at the base of Proudhon's philosophy of social justice.

"M. Proudhon," he says, "has of the dialectic of Hegel nothing but the language." He has only the "sacramental formula."[22] He has failed to comprehend the real meaning of the dialectical idea, which looks to the overcoming of all dualism, all contradiction. Proudhon, says Marx elsewhere apropos of the same point, is the true petty bourgeois. He is "composed of On The One Hand and On The Other Hand. . . . It is so in his morals, in everything. He is a living contradiction." Further, "one finds in him a *dualism* between life and ideas, soul and body, a dualism which recurs in many forms."[23] This is the nub of the issue. Proudhon's philosophy of justice is dualistic in essence. It assumes that antagonistic duality, situations of conflict between two parties or two principles, are inherent in life, especially in social life, and it looks to the establishment of equilibrium, to a delimitation of mutual claims. Marx, too, sees that human life is shot through with situations of conflict, with *Lebenskollisionen*, as he sometimes calls them. Unlike Proudhon, however, he regards this fact as profoundly abnormal, even intolerable, and his prescription, accordingly, is radically opposed to Proudhon's.

> In his desire to reconcile the contradictions, Monsieur Proudhon does not even ask himself if the basis of those contradictions must not itself be overthrown. . . . All he is looking for is a new formula by which to establish an equilibrium between these forces.[24]

To Proudhonian justice as equilibrium of antagonisms Marx opposed revolution as abolition of antagonisms. He wanted to overthrow the "basis of those contradictions," to uproot conflict at the source, to eliminate the conflict situation. His philosophy expressed a search for unity—for a world beyond all antagonisms and therefore beyond justice as equilibrium of them.

22. *The Poverty of Philosophy*, pp. 115, 122.
23. *Selected Correspondence*, pp. 17, 176.
24. *Ibid.*, p. 16.

Chapter Three

THE POLITICAL THEORY OF CLASSICAL MARXISM

◇◇◇◇◇◇◇◇◇◇◇◇◇◇◇◇◇◇◇◇◇◇◇◇◇◇◇◇

That Marx ranks among the major political theorists is a widely accepted opinion in our time. The histories of political thought commonly accord him a chapter or two, and the great age of political theory in the modern West is often viewed as running from Machiavelli to Marx. With the reservation that Marx's impact upon political thought may have been greater than his measurable contribution to it warranted, I see no reason to take issue with this view.

As one of the "greats" of Western political thought, Marx was in some ways a great dissenter. He radically rejected the civilization of which he was so much a part. He saw the state as coercive power wielded in the interests of property, and its legitimation was no part of his intellectual concern. Nevertheless, Marx's political theory was closer to at least one main current in the classical Western tradition than might be supposed. A long line of eminent political thinkers, including Aristotle, Machiavelli, Locke, and James Madison, had preceded him in offering an economic interpretation of politics, in linking the state with class interest and the property system.[1]

If justification is needed for returning to such familiar territory as Marx's political thought, it may lie in certain characteristic inadequacies of past treatments of this subject. First, exposition of the Marxist conception of history as a whole has loomed large in these accounts, and systematic analysis of the political aspect of Marxist theory has correspondingly suffered.[2] Secondly, Marx's political thought has mistakenly been equated with his theory of the state, which is only a part of it. And thirdly, his descriptive theory of the state has been emphasized to the neglect of his normative view, his position as a political philosopher. These comments define the tasks of the present chapter. Starting with an analysis of the theory of the state in classical Marxism, I will go on to present the thesis that the theory of the state, for all its importance in Marxist political theory, is not the whole of it and not even the most vital part, since Marx sees the economy as the prime historical locus of the political relationship between man and man. In conclusion I will attempt to formulate Marx's position as a political philosopher, dealing in particular with the philosophical relation between Marxism and anarchism.

1. On this point, see, for example, Charles A. Beard, *The Economic Basis of Politics and Related Writings* (New York: Vintage Books, 1957), ch. 3.
2. The chapter on "Marx and Dialectical Materialism" in George Sabine's *A History of Political Theory* (New York: Henry Holt, 1950) is an illustration. There are, of course, exceptions, a notable one being John Plamenatz's systematic analysis of the political views of Marx and Engels in Ch. 6 of *Man and Society* (New York and San Francisco: McGraw-Hill, 1963), II.

The State as Alienated Social Power

We find in the writings of Marx and Engels a twofold view of the nature of the state. On the one hand, they give the well-known functional definition of it as "an organization of the possessing class for its protection against the non-possessing class."[3] On the other hand, the state is also defined in intrinsic terms as an embodiment in a special class of governors—politicians, bureaucracy, standing army, police, etc. —of society's power. As Marx puts it, "by the word 'state' is meant the government machine, or the state insofar as it forms a special organism separated from society through the division of labor. . . ."[4]

In so characterizing the state, Marx was expressing a view that he had developed in the formative period of his thought. On the road to his first formulation of the materialist conception of history in the Paris manuscripts of 1844, he had briefly applied himself to political theory. In 1843 he produced an unfinished critical commentary on Hegel's *Philosophy of Right,* and some published articles summarizing the results. Applying a method of inversion of Hegelianism which he had learned from Ludwig Feuerbach, he constructed a theory of the political life as a sphere of man's alienation. Feuerbach had extracted from Hegelianism by his method of inversion the view that religious, i.e., God-oriented, man was man alienated from himself; for God was only an imaginary externalization of man's own idealized attributes.

Just so, reasoned Marx, man as citizen in the modern state, i.e., as a communal being or member of the political com-

---

3. Engels, *The Origin of the Family, Private Property and the State,* in Marx and Engels, *Selected Works,* II, 291.
4. "Critique of the Gotha Program," in Marx and Engels, *Selected Works,* II, 31.

munity, is but an idealization of real man and hence an "abstraction." Real man is not man qua citizen but man as a member of civil society (*bürgerliche Gesellschaft*), which Hegel himself, influenced by such thinkers as Adam Smith, represented as the arena of an economic war of all against all. Accordingly, the primary realm of human existence is the economy rather than the polity. Hegel's error was to treat the state as the foundation of civil society, whereas the truth is just the reverse: civil society is the foundation of the state. And the state, like Feuerbach's God, is an externalization of the powers of the species. It has a real material existence, however, rather than a purely imaginary one in heaven. It exists as a special political organism separate from the rest of society and lording it over the latter. To overcome political alienation, therefore, man must respossess this alienated social power by revolutionary means. For "only when man recognizes and organizes his '*forces propres*' as *social* forces and so ceases to separate social power from himself in the form of *political* power—only then will human emancipation take place."[5]

As already indicated above, Marx's early image of the state as alienated social power, a creature of society that comes to dominate its creator, persists in mature Marxism. Once historically established, writes Engels, political power is "endowed with a movement of its own" and "strives for as much independence as possible."[6] Marx, for his part, describes the "special organism" of political rule as a parasitic growth on the social body. Speaking, for example, of the executive power in nineteenth-century France, "with its

5. Marx, "Zur Judenfrage," in *Die Frühschriften*, ed. Siegfried Landshut (Stuttgart: Alfred Kröner Verlag, 1953), p. 199. For a fuller exposition of this argument, see *Philosophy and Myth in Karl Marx*, pp. 102–105. Marx's own recollection of his thought-process in the critical commentary on Hegel is contained in his preface to *The Critique of Political Economy*.

6. Letter to C. Schmidt of Oct. 27, 1890, in *Selected Correspondence*, p. 480.

artificial state machinery embracing wide strata, with a host of officials numbering half a million, besides an army of another half million," he depicts this power as an "appalling parasitic growth, which enmeshes the body of French society like a net and chokes all the pores. . . ."[7] In a similar vein, Engels pictures the United States as a politician-ridden nation where "two great gangs of political speculators" alternate in power and at the public trough. "Nowhere do 'politicians' form a more separate and powerful section of the nation than precisely in North America," he elaborates. "It is precisely in America that we see best how there takes place this process of the state power making itself independent in relation to society, whose mere instrument it was originally intended to be."[8]

These remarks of Engels appear in his preface to a twentieth-anniversary edition of Marx's pamphlet on the Paris Commune of 1871, *The Civil War in France*, and reflect one of its chief themes. Indeed, all that the two men wrote about the Commune calls for interpretation in the light of classical Marxism's conception of the state as alienated social power. They saw in the Commune a revolutionary movement to destroy the state as, in Marx's words, a "parasitic excrescence" on the body of society, and this was a reason for their rapturous response. The Commune, wrote Engels, signified a "shattering" (*Sprengung*) of the former state power. By filling all posts through elections on the basis of universal suffrage and by paying all officials, high or low, only the wages received by other workers, the Commune inaugurated the reversal of the historical transformation of the state and its organs from servants of society into masters of society.[9] This echoed what Marx had said twenty years before. "While the merely repressive

---

7. *The Eighteenth Brumaire*, p. 107.
8. Introduction to Marx, *The Civil War in France*, in Marx and Engels, *Selected Works*, I, 483, 484.
9. *Ibid.*, p. 484.

organs of the old governmental power were to be amputated," he had written of the Commune, "its legitimate functions were to be wrested from an authority usurping preeminence over society itself, and restored to the responsible agents of society. . . . The Communal Constitution would have restored to the social body all the forces hitherto absorbed by the state parasite feeding upon and clogging the free movement of society."[10] For Marx, the Commune was an unsuccessful but portentous first attempt by man in the mass to repossess his alienated *"forces propres"* and abrogate the historic externalization of social power into the state.

There appears to exist if not an outright contradiction, then at any rate a definite tension in the thought of Marx and Engels between their conception of the state as alienated social power and their functional definition of it as an organ of class rule. Whereas the one view propounds a dichotomy of state versus society, the other treats the state as the instrumentality of a class, which in turn is a *part* of society. How, then, is it possible to conceive the state as an entity "independent" of society and lording it over the latter? The two men seem to have been somewhat uneasily aware of this problem. Engels offered a partial solution in the hypothesis that the state acquires a certain independence of society at times when no one class is clearly dominant. Citing as examples the absolute monarchies of the seventeenth and eighteenth centuries, which held the balance between nobility and bourgeoisie, and the Bonapartism of the first and second French empires, which played off the proletariat against the bourgeoisie and vice versa, Engels offered the generalization that there are periods when "the warring classes balance each other so nearly that the state power, as ostensible mediator, acquires, for the moment, a certain degree of independence of both."[11] This, however, would

10. *The Civil War in France, op. cit.*, pp. 520, 521.
11. *Origin of the Family, op. cit.*, p. 290.

at best explain only certain instances of something that Marx and Engels elsewhere in their writings describe as a universal historical tendency, and the tension between their two approaches to the state went unresolved.

The State as Organized Coercion

Inverting Hegel's political philosophy in his critical commentary of 1843, Marx postulated that civil society was the foundation of the state and economics the foundation of civil society. He thereby arrived at the first premise of historical materialism, on the primacy of economics in human affairs. The deeper existential significance of this familiar Marxist tenet becomes apparent only in the full context of the materialist conception of history as Marx went on to expound it in his Paris manuscripts of 1844 and then in Part I of *The German Ideology* (1845–46). Man, in Marx's image of him, is essentially a producing animal who has his historical being primarily in the realm of material production. The growth-process of the human species is in substance a process of man's production of the world of material objects that surrounds him. And history being chiefly a production process, human society itself is basically a society of production—a set of social relations that men enter in their productive activity. In a well-known later formulation of historical materialism, Marx called these social relations of production the "basis" of society. All other institutions and forms of consciousness, including political institutions and political consciousness, he relegated to the social "superstructure" arising over this foundation.[12]

---

12. "Preface to *The Critique of Political Economy*," in Marx and Engels, *Selected Works*, I, 363.

Marx's theory goes on to assert that the human society of production has been deeply divided throughout recorded history. The social relations of production have been so many different forms of a "social division of labor" between a minority class of nonproducing owners of the means of production and a majority class of nonowning producers. Every social system based on the division of labor is necessarily, moreover, a conflictual system. The social division of labor is not simply a division but an antagonism, and class-divided society is society in conflict. What makes it so, according to Marx, is a rebelliousness of man as producer against his life-conditions in societies of production based on division of labor. The rebelliousness is explained by the inability of man as producer to develop his productive powers freely and to the full within any given social division of labor. Thus bourgeois man could not develop the new capitalist productive powers freely within the division of labor between lords and serfs and the feudal system of landed property. And now proletarian man, in Marx's view, is increasingly restive owing to the inability to freely develop the new productive powers of modern machine industry within the division of labor between capitalist and worker, i.e., within the confines of wage labor as the mode of production. Generalizing, we may say that for classical Marxism the rebelliousness of man as producer is a constant historical tendency which periodically rises to a peak of intensity, bursts out in a revolutionary upheaval, and then subsides—but not for long—with the resulting transformation of society. The envisaged destination of the historical process is a classless society, in which the social relations of production will no longer take the form of division of labor, and hence will not become again a fetter upon man's powers of production.

The state, a key element in the social superstructure, is functionally defined for Marx and Engels in this theoretical context. It institutionalizes the conflict-situation in societies founded on division of labor in production, and so is "simply the official form of the antagonism in civil society."[13] The state, according to this view, is an instrumentality for waging the class struggle *from above*. The possessing class, as the beneficiary of an existing social order of production, will necessarily resist all efforts of the producer class to transform society. In doing so it will freely make use of organized coercion. To curb the ever-rebellious producers and protect the social order from the danger of overthrow, it will use the police, the prisons, the standing army, the courts, etc. The state is thus seen by classical Marxism as fundamentally a repressive force. In Engels' words,

> the state of antiquity was above all the state of the slave owners for the purpose of *holding down* the slaves, as the feudal state was the organ of the nobility for *holding down* the peasant serfs and bondsmen, and the modern representative state is an instrument of exploitation of wage labor by capital.[14]

In the work from which this passage is quoted, Engels also writes that the state historically arose as a force for keeping class conflict within certain tolerable bounds. In order that antagonistic classes might not consume themselves and society in sterile struggle, he says, "a power seemingly standing above society became necessary for the purpose of moderating the conflict, of keeping it within the bounds of 'order'. . . ."[15] This statement must be kept in context to avoid misinterpretation. Engels does not mean that the state stands above class conflict, but only that it

---

13. Marx, *The Poverty of Philosophy*, p. 190.
14. *Origin of the Family*, in Marx and Engels, *Selected Works*, II, 290. Italics added.
15. *Ibid.*, p. 289.

seems to. Nor does he mean that the state is in essence a conflict-preventing or conflict-resolving force. Along with Marx, he sees the state as a *weapon* of class conflict, but a weapon which, in the hands of the economically dominant class, is employed to prevent the underlying antagonism in the society from exploding into revolutionary violence. Only in this special sense does the state, in the Marxist theory of it, exist as a means of "moderating" conflict in society.

For Marx and Engels, the social history of man is a series of systemic conflicts in which the fundamental issue has been the social order itself—its preservation or its overthrow. The division of labor has bifurcated society to such an extent that the great question for every historical society has always been: how long can it hold itself together? And the Marxist view of the state is governed by this underlying assumption about society. The repressive function that it assigns to state power arises logically out of the imperative needs of society as a conflictual system whose very persistence is always at stake. The state is the supreme defense mechanism of a threatened social structure, and a mechanism that is regularly having to be used, violently, because the internal threat to the system, for the reasons already explained, is continually manifesting itself in violent ways. Hence Lenin caught the spirit of classical Marxism, and was merely accentuating a basic theme of its political theory, when he defined the state as "organized and systematic violence."[16]

Marx's theory holds that class struggles, when they grow in intensity, become political struggles. The possessing class is ready to call out the police and the army at the slightest provocation from the producers. And by the same token,

16. *The State and Revolution*, in V. I. Lenin, *Selected Works* (Moscow: Foreign Languages Publishing House, 1946–1947), II, 197.

the producers cannot fight their class struggles without pitting themselves against the existing state. Since the state is the social structure's defense mechanism, they cannot revolutionize the social order without overthrowing the state and taking political power. The producers cannot transform the social foundation without tearing down the old political superstructure. So Marx's political theory holds that all social revolutions necessitate political revolutions. It sees the French Revolution, for example, as the political expression of the deeper bourgeois revolution in French society. But the "Thermidor" too finds its explanation, for Marx, in the tendency of every revolutionary new form of statehood to become very quickly a conservative force, a repressive defense mechanism for *its* social order. The state qua state is thus seen as in essence a conservative force for preservation of the social status quo. The later Leninist notion of the communist party-state as a force for social change, an instrumentality of a long-range revolutionary transformation of society from above, is in this respect a serious modification of Marxist theory and represents one of the significant points of divergence between classical and communist Marxism.

It follows that Marx and Engels propounded an economic interpretation of politics in both a radical and special form. Politics, on their view, is fundamentally *about* economics as defined above, i.e., about modes and relations of production and their changes. They were well aware, of course, that this conception ran counter to the general assumption of participants in political life, and of those who have written about it, that political history genuinely revolves around political and moral issues, such as constitutions, forms of state, human rights, the franchise, and justice. To account for the discrepancy between the real meaning of politics and what people believe about it, Marx and Engels invoked their theory of ideological thinking as false consciousness. Not only did all class conflicts tend to take the form of political struggles; all political conflicts were class struggles in *ideological disguise*. Such ideological disguise of economic issues as political ones was a matter of genuine obfuscation in the heads of men, including political leaders. Thus the struggles in states between government and opposition were manifestations of class conflict. But class conflict was reflected "in inverted form, no longer directly but indirectly, not as a class struggle but as a fight for political principles, and so distorted that it has taken us thousands of years to get behind it."[17] In the same vein, Marx wrote that "all struggles within the state, the struggle between democracy, aristocracy and monarchy, the struggle for the franchise, etc., etc., are merely the illusory forms in which the real struggles of the different classes are fought out among one another."[18] Elsewhere, in answering the objection that his economic interpretation of politics would not apply to ancient Greece and Rome, where political considerations really were the dominant ones, he declared that classical antiquity could no more live on politics than the Middle Ages could live on Catholicism, and went on: ". . . a very little knowledge of the history of the Roman republic suffices to acquaint us with the fact that the secret core of its history is formed by the history of the system of landed proprietorship."[19]

So political consciousness became, for classical Marxism, a form of false consciousness, an upside-down view of reality, and commonsense assumptions about political life were explained away as illusions. Marx's thinking in this regard presupposed a distinction between "manifest" and "latent" meaning. Political consciousness was in a manifest sense about moral-political issues, but latently it was about eco-

17. Engels, Letter to C. Schmidt of Oct. 27, 1890, *loc. cit.*
18. *The German Ideology*, p. 23.
19. *Capital*, p. 57 n.

nomic ones. The underlying meaning of politics, obscure to participants and scholars alike, lay in the basic inner conflicts in the human society of production, the conflicts over modes of productive activity.

Historical Forms of the State

Much of what Marx and Engels wrote about the state was expressed in sweeping generalities typified by the *Communist Manifesto's* description of the state as "merely the organized power of one class for oppressing another." To what extent were they conscious of differences between forms of government, and what importance did they attach to them? For reasons already touched on, they were much more impressed by that which all forms of government have in common than by the features distinguishing one form from another. They were not, however, oblivious to differences and did not treat them as insignificant. Though this aspect of their political theory was never systematically elaborated in detail, they did propound a kind of Marxist "comparative politics."

Not surprisingly in view of the general historical structure of their thought, this was a comparative politics over time rather than across space. They tended, in other words, to assume that each successive epoch in the social history of mankind, each dominant socioeconomic formation, has its own characteristic form of statehood. On that basis there should be five different forms of government corresponding to the five forms of class society mentioned by Marx: Asiatic society, the slaveowning society of classical antiquity, feudal society, modern bourgeois society, and future communist society in its lower phase during which the state would persist in the form of a "dictatorship of the proletariat." But Marx and Engels dealt only very sketchily with the theme of the correlations between the types of class-divided society and the forms of government.

Influenced by the writings of British political economists, notably Richard Jones and John Stuart Mill, Marx saw Asiatic society as a socioeconomic formation based on irrigated agriculture. Since the obligation of seeing to the construction and maintenance of complex and costly canals and waterworks devolved upon the state in those conditions, the centralizing power of government expanded very greatly and the state took the form of "Oriental despotism." Marx had little further to say on the social order of Oriental despotism.[20] Nor did he and Engels designate a particular form of government as characteristic of the slaveowning society of classical antiquity—an omission that may find its explanation in the diversity of forms of government in ancient Greece and Rome. They saw monarchy as the typical political form of feudal society, however, and parliamentary democracy, variously called the "representative state" or "democratic republic," as the form of government proper to a capitalist society in its mature development. It was in this "last form of state of bourgeois society" that the class struggle was destined to be "fought out to a conclusion."[21]

The attitude of Marx and Engels toward the political institutions of liberal parliamentary democracy was ambivalent. On the one hand, they saw the democratic republic in

20. See his article on "The British Rule in India" (in Marx and Engels, *Selected Works*) for his views on this subject. In an essay on "The Ruling Bureaucracy of Oriental Despotism: A Phenomenon That Paralyzed Marx" (*The Review of Politics*, July, 1953), Karl A. Wittfogel hypothesized that Marx's reticence on this theme stemmed from a reluctance to discuss the class structure of Oriental society, and suggested that this in turn expressed a fear of conveying the thought that a bureaucracy might prove the ruling and owning class again in a future socialist society. This is at best a highly speculative explanation, particularly considering that Oriental society was not the only prebourgeois social formation concerning which Marx had relatively little to say. The only form of society that Marx showed any interest in analyzing in systematic detail was, after all, bourgeois society.

21. Marx, "Critique of the Gotha Program," in Marx and Engels, *Selected Works*, II, 31.

bourgeois society as being, like all previous forms of the state, a class dictatorship. The liberal democratic state was a camouflaged "bourgeois dictatorship."[22] Its representative government and universal suffrage meant no more than the opportunity of "deciding once in three or six years which member of the ruling class was to misrepresent the people in parliament."[23] Yet Marx and Engels were not inclined to dismiss democratic political institutions as useless or unimportant. Rather, they saw in them a school of political training for the working class in bourgeois society, a stimulus to the growth of revolutionary class consciousness in the proletariat. For the debate by which parliamentary democracy lived could not but spread to the larger society outside:

> The parliamentary regime leaves everything to the decision of majorities; how shall the great majorities outside parliament not want to decide? When you play the fiddle at the top of the state, what else is to be expected but that those down below dance?[24]

But was it possible, as later social democratic Marxists came to believe, for an anticapitalist revolution and socialist transformation of bourgeois society to take place in a peaceful and orderly way through the electoral process in a parliamentary democracy? Could the workers achieve political power by democratic means and proceed by those means to change the mode of production? On one or two occasions Marx alluded to such a possibility, most notably when he allowed in a speech in Amsterdam in 1872 that in England and America, and possibly in Holland as well, the workers might conceivably attain their revolutionary aim

22. Marx, *The Class Struggles in France*, p. 58.
23. Marx, *The Civil War in France*, in Marx and Engels, *Selected Works*, I, 520.
24. Marx, *The Eighteenth Brumaire*, p. 58.

by peaceful means.[25] But it is uncertain how seriously he or Engels actually entertained such a belief, which was at variance with a fundamental tendency of their thought over the years. Addressing himself in 1874 to believers in a non-authoritarian revolution, Engels inquired: "Have these gentlemen ever seen a revolution?" And he went on:

A revolution is certainly the most authoritarian thing there is; it is the act whereby one part of the population imposes its will upon the other part by means of rifles, bayonets, and cannon—authoritarian means, if such there be at all. . . .[26]

It is true that later, in his 1895 introduction to a new edition of Marx's *Class Struggles in France*, Engels found the social democratic movement to be thriving on universal suffrage and the ballot-box. But even there he did not assert that the working class could actually come to power by these means. He said nothing to suggest that he had altered the view, expressed some years earlier, that universal suffrage was not, and could not be, anything more than a "gauge of the maturity of the working class." Its mission was to herald the revolutionary *dénouement*: "On the day the thermometer of universal suffrage registers boiling point among the workers, both they and the capitalists will know what to do."[27]

Marx and Engels saw in the class state not only organized coercion but also an element of deception. In each of its historical incarnations the state had been the dictatorship of

25. Quoted in Karl Kautsky, *The Dictatorship of the Proletariat* (Ann Arbor: University of Michigan Press, 1964), p. 10. See also Marx's article "The Chartists," *New York Daily Tribune*, August 25, 1852, suggesting that in England universal suffrage must inevitably result in the political supremacy of the working class.

26. "On Authority," in Marx and Engels, *Selected Works*, I, 639.

27. *Origin of the Family*, in Marx and Engels, *Selected Works*, II, 291.

a minority class of owners of the means of production. But its class character had been camouflaged. In Europe, for example, monarchy had been "the normal incumbrance and indispensable cloak of class-rule."[28] And the modern democratic republic claimed to be a state ruled by the people as a whole through their elected representatives in parliament; the control of this state by the capitalist class, and their use of it for class purposes, was concealed. This theme of the manipulation of political forms to cover up minority class rule is a minor one in Marx and Engels, but merits special attention because it influenced later elitist theories of the state. In the elitist theories of the sociologists Gaetano Mosca and Vilfredo Pareto, the ruling class is no longer defined in Marx's manner, and the possibility of a future society without a ruling class is explicitly or implicitly denied. But notwithstanding the fact that the elitists were anti-Marxists and offered their view of the state in part as a rebuttal of Marx's, their thinking showed the impact of classical Marxist political theory. Pareto admitted as much when he praised the "sociological part" of Marx's teaching, the idea that societies are divided into classes of rulers and ruled.[29] This basic notion, along with the tendency to see minority class rule as something concealed behind external political forms, is something for which the elitist theory is largely indebted to Marx. And it may be through this channel that Marx has had his most enduring influence upon political thought in the contemporary West.

So strong was Marx's belief in the class essence of every historical form of the state that the reality of autocracy or personal rule at certain junctures in history seems to have escaped him. Engels, as noted earlier, suggested in one pas-

28. Marx, *The Civil War in France, op. cit.*, p. 522.
29. Quoted in H. Stuart Hughes, *Consciousness and Society: The Reconstruction of European Social Thought 1890–1930* (New York: Vintage Books, 1961), pp. 79–80.

sage that there were times when autocratic rulers might have become independent powers owing to a balance of contending classes in society. Marx, however, was less inclined to think in this fashion. The point is best illustrated by his interpretation of the rule of Louis Bonaparte. France, Marx wrote, seemed to have escaped the despotism of a class only to fall back beneath the despotism of an individual. But it was not so: "Bonaparte represents a class, and the most numerous class of French society at that, the *small peasants*." The small peasants were not, though, a unified class, and since they were incapable for this reason of cognizing and enforcing their class interest in their own name, they had to do it through a representative:

> Their representative must at the same time appear as their master, as an authority over them, as an unlimited governmental power, that protects them against the other classes and sends them the rain and the sunshine from above. The political influence of the small peasants, therefore, finds its final expression in the executive power subordinating society to itself.[30]

It was an ingenious interpretation but also an arbitrary one, reflecting Marx's incapacity to grasp government under any other aspect than that of rule on behalf of the economic interest of a social class. I am unable to agree with Professor John Plamenatz, therefore, when he writes that Marx, in the *Eighteenth Brumaire of Louis Bonaparte*, showed an understanding of the phenomenon that later came to be known as fascism and, in particular, that "he saw that classless adventurers could, by playing off the classes against one another, capture the State and use it to promote interests which were not class interests."[31] It seems, on the contrary, that Marx's interpretation of Louis Bona-

---

30. *The Eighteenth Brumaire*, p. 109.
31. *Man and Society*, II, 371, 372.

parte as the political representative of an inarticulate small peasantry foreshadowed the grievous mistake of Marxism in the twentieth century when it interpreted the full-grown fascisms of Hitler and Mussolini as forms of class rule by the monopoly bourgeoisie. One of the serious deficiencies of Marxist political theory is the difficulty that it inevitably encounters when it takes up the problem of personal dictatorship. The continuing absence of a "Marxist" explanation of Stalin and Stalinism is only one of many manifestations of this deficiency.

The Proletarian State

Marx and Engels thought the state would disappear in the higher phase of the communist society. But in the transitional lower phase of communist society—society as it would exist in the aftermath of proletarian revolution—the state would survive as a dictatorship of the working class. The *Communist Manifesto* thus speaks of the proletariat constituting itself as the ruling class. In *The Class Struggles in France*, written in 1850, Marx proclaimed

> the class dictatorship of the revolution, the class dictatorship of the proletariat as the inevitable transit point to the abolition of class differences generally, to the abolition of all the productive relations on which they rest, to the abolition of all the social relations that correspond to these relations of production, to the revolutionizing of all the ideas that result from these social connections.[32]

Returning to the theme in a letter of 1852 to his friend Joseph Weydemeyer, Marx declared that "the class struggle

32. *The Class Struggles in France*, p. 126.

necessarily leads to the dictatorship of the proletariat" and that "this dictatorship itself constitutes only the transition to the *abolition* of all classes and to a *classless society*."[33] Finally, in his unpublished notes of 1875 on the Gotha Program, Marx wrote:

> Between capitalist and communist society lies the period of the revolutionary transformation of the one into the other. There corresponds to this also a political transition period in which the state can be nothing but *the revolutionary dictatorship of the proletariat.*[34]

The doctrine of proletarian dictatorship is beyond question an integral part of classical Marxism and its political theory. On the other hand, Marx and Engels were not inclined to go into detail on this theme and left somewhat unclear how they concretely envisaged the future proletarian dictatorship. This paved the way for later Marxist controversy over the question. Although diverse schools of Marxist thought have recognized the doctrine of the proletarian dictatorship as an inalienable part of Marxism, they have differed, at times very deeply and bitterly, over the amount of importance to be attached to it and the proper interpretation to be placed upon it. Indeed, the theoretical and practical question of what the proletarian dictatorship would and should look like in practice, and the related question of what the founders believed on the point, directly underlay the great schism of 1917 and after between orthodox social democratic Marxism and the communist Marxism of Lenin and his followers. The issue was whether or not the latter were acting as good Marxists in setting up the Soviet one-party state and calling it a Marxist "dictatorship of the proletariat." In an effort to prove in advance that this *would* be a valid Marxist action, Lenin in the summer of 1917

33. *Selected Correspondence*, p. 57.
34. Marx and Engels, *Selected Works*, II, 30.

wrote *The State and Revolution,* his principal contribution to Marxist political theory. The doctrinal conflict was joined when Karl Kautsky published a Marxist criticism of the Bolshevik Revolution in his pamphlet of August, 1918, *The Dictatorship of the Proletariat,* to which Lenin later responded with *The Proletarian Revolution and the Renegade Kautsky.*

In attacking the Russian Bolsheviks on Marxist grounds for setting up a dictatorial regime and ruling by force and violence in the name of the proletariat, Kautsky contended that democracy and Marxist socialism were inseparable. A Marxist dictatorship of the proletariat would not be a dictatorship in the "literal sense" of suspension of democracy and rule by a single person. It would be class rule by the proletariat and, as such, it would be majority rule according to the generally accepted democratic procedures and with full protection of minorities. In the proletarian context, therefore, the term "dictatorship" was to be understood in a Pickwickian sense as referring *not* to a form of government but rather to "a condition which must everywhere arise when the proletariat has conquered political power," *viz.,* the condition of proletarian "sovereignty" in a society composed in the majority of proletarians. And to prove that this was the Marx-Engels viewpoint as well as his own, Kautsky cited Marx's description of the Paris Commune, in *The Civil War in France,* as a polity that abolished a standing army and state officialdom and operated on the basis of general suffrage and citizen rotation in elective public office. Had not Marx himself called the Commune an essentially working-class government? And had not Engels, in his preface to a twentieth-anniversary edition of Marx's famous pamphlet, expressly held up the Commune as the first example of a dictatorship of the proletariat?[35]

35. *The Dictatorship of the Proletariat,* pp. 30, 43–44, 46.

Testimony could thus be found for a social democratic interpretation of the founders' views on the proletarian dictatorship. Marx did portray the Commune as a libertarian new order, and hailed it as "the political form at last discovered under which to work out the economic emancipation of labor."[36] Nor was this the only evidence in support of the Kautskyan case. The *Communist Manifesto* had, after all, described the predicted future establishment of proletarian class rule as the "winning of democracy" (*Erkampfung der Demokratie*). And much later, in his criticism of the draft of the program to be adopted by the German Social Democratic Party at its Erfurt Congress, Engels wrote that the working class could come to power only under the form of the democratic republic, and added: "This is even the specific form for the dictatorship of the proletariat, as the great French revolution has already shown."[37]

Yet the Kautskyan interpretation of the founders' position was ultimately shaky and unconvincing, for it ignored important conflicting evidence. The very words of Engels just quoted show the untenability of Kautsky's view that Marx and Engels conceived the proletarian dictatorship not as a form of government but as a "condition" only. They saw it as the final form that the state was destined to take in history. And Engels' reference to the French Revolution in this context is only one of many indications that the political *content* of the proletarian dictatorship, even within the frame of a democratic republic, was envisaged in a very different manner from Kautsky's as described above. There is adequate evidence to show that when Marx and Engels spoke of the future proletarian dictatorship, they were not using the term "dictatorship" in a merely Pickwickian sense but literally. It is true that they offered no such general definition of the term as Lenin's, according to which "dic-

36. *The Civil War in France, op. cit.,* p. 522.
37. *Selected Correspondence,* p. 486.

tatorship is rule based directly upon force and unrestricted by any laws." Nor were they as explicit on the applicability of the general formula to the case of the proletarian state as Lenin was when he added: "The revolutionary dictatorship of the proletariat is rule won and maintained by the use of violence by the proletariat against the bourgeoisie, rule that is unrestricted by any laws."[38] Yet this appears to have been the direction of their thinking.

One of the indications of it is their critical reaction to the draft Gotha Program's call for a "free people's state." They objected to the idea that a "free state" should be a stated goal of the workers' party in Germany, and did so on the explicit ground that a proletarian state could no more be a free one than any other form of state could. "As, there-fore, the state is only a transitional institution which is used in the struggle, in the revolution, in order to hold down one's adversaries by force," declared Engels in his letter to Bebel of March 18–28, 1875, about the draft Program, "it is pure nonsense to talk of a free people's state: so long as the proletariat still *uses* the state, it does not use it in the inter-ests of freedom but in order to hold down its adversaries, and as soon as it becomes possible to speak of freedom the state as such ceases to exist."[39] Like all previous historical forms of the state, the proletarian state was looked upon by the founders of Marxism as an instrumentality of class struggle, a means of "holding down" a class in society, a repressive force. Nor did they shrink, even in their mature years, from the corollary that the revolutionary dictatorship of the proletariat would have to resort to the weapon of terror. Engels insisted on the need for a revolution to main-tain itself in power by means of terror, and criticized the Communards of 1871 for not having done so resolutely

38. *The Proletarian Revolution and the Renegade Kautsky*, in Lenin, *Selected Works*, II, 365.
39. *Selected Correspondence*, p. 337.

enough. Could the Commune have lasted a single day, he inquired, without resorting to the "authority of the armed people" against the bourgeoisie? And: "Should we not, on the contrary, reproach it for not having used it freely enough?"[40] And Marx, stating in a letter of 1881 that the majority of the Commune was in no sense socialist, made clear what, in his view, a genuinely socialist government should be prepared to do on assuming power:

> One thing you can at any rate be sure of: a socialist government does not come into power in a country unless conditions are so developed that it can above all take the necessary measures for intimidating the mass of the bourgeoisie sufficiently to gain time—the first *desideratum*—for lasting action.[41]

All this speaks against one further argument that has been adduced in favor of the social democratic exegesis of classical Marxism on the proletarian dictatorship. The argument holds that the thinking of Marx and Engels underwent a democratic evolution over the years, that they moved from a youthful Blanquist tendency or Jacobinism in 1848 and its aftermath to a mature outlook that was sober, moderate, and genuinely democratic. According to the Russian Menshevik leader Julius Martov, for example, Marx and Engels originally conceived the idea of proletarian dictatorship in the late 1840's under the influence of the Jacobin tradition of 1793, with its minority political dictatorship and the Terror. But later, as Marx and Engels became convinced that conscious support of the majority of the population was required for a socialist revolution, their conception of the proletarian dictatorship lost its Jacobin content and they

40. "On Authority," in Marx and Engels, *Selected Works*, I, 639.
41. Letter to Domela Nieuwenhuis of February 22, 1881, in *Selected Correspondence*, p. 386.

envisaged proletarian class rule "only in the forms of a total democracy."[42]

The weakness of this line of argument is clear from testimony already cited above. Although the mature Marx and Engels were not the flaming revolutionists that they had been in their youth, they remained faithful to the Marxian revolutionary idea and vision. It is true that they envisaged proletarian rule as a majoritarian dictatorship, but it is also true, as we have just had occasion to observe, that democratic protection of the rights of the class minority was no part of their image of it. In their later as well as their earlier years, they saw the class rule of the proletariat as essentially a regime of revolution (a "class dictatorship of the revolution," as Marx had called it). They took it for granted that as such it would have bourgeois class enemies whom the government of the proletarian majority would have to deal with—and in their view ought to deal with—by forcible means, not excluding terror. The proletarian government, like every other, would be repressive in nature.

Lenin was on strong textual ground in emphasizing this point in the controversy with social democratic Marxism. But that is not to say that his exegesis of the doctrine of proletarian dictatorship was correct in all details or even in all essentials. If Kautsky unduly deprecated the significance of this doctrine in classical Marxism, Lenin vastly overrated it. Not content with saying in *The State and Revolution* that to be a genuine Marxist one had to accept not only the class struggle but also the proletarian dictatorship as its outcome, he subsequently asserted that the conception of proletarian dictatorship was "the essence of Marx's doctrine" and "sums up the whole of his revolutionary teach-

42. Julius Martov, *The State and The Socialist Revolution* (New York, 1939), pp. 57, 63. The lingering influence of this line of argument in present-day Marx scholarship in the West is to be seen in George Lichtheim, *Marxism: An Historical and Critical Survey* (New York: Praeger, 1961).

ing."[43] This was to blow up one important part of Marx's thought out of all true proportion. Furthermore, if Kautsky overly "democratized" Marx's notion of the proletarian dictatorship, Lenin too construed it in a manner that Marx had not foreseen. There is nothing, for example, to indicate that Marx conceived the proletarian state as a party-state, a dictatorship of a single party ruling, or claiming to rule, *on behalf* of the proletariat. Nor did he picture it in Leninist fashion as a form of polity destined to endure through an entire historical epoch of transition to communism; for the transition itself was understood in different terms. Precisely because the proletarian state would be a regime of the immense majority in an advanced society, a majority in the process of abolishing private property and therewith the division of labor in production, it would soon lose its repressive *raison d'etre* and wither away. As a "dictatorship of the revolution," it would have a short life at the close of man's prehistory. Such, at any rate, is the belief that Marx and Engels seem to have entertained.

The Economy as Polity

To our conventional way of thinking, Marx's political theory is summed up in the views treated in the foregoing pages. But the conventional view is misleading in this instance. Marx's theory of the state is an extremely important portion of his political theory, and the part that has directly influenced the subsequent course of political thought. Yet a philosophical appreciation of Marx as a political thinker cannot rest at this point. It must proceed to examine the political aspect of his economic thought.

43. Lenin, *Selected Works*, II, 163, 362.

What, parenthetically, is political theory about? One answer would be that it is about the state, since most systematic political theorizing has addressed itself to questions concerning the origin, nature, functions, and limits of the state. Alternatively, one can say that the proper subject-matter of political theory is the realm of the political, which includes the state but at the same time greatly transcends it. The "realm of the political" may in turn be defined as the realm of power and authority relations among people. Such relations between man as ruler and man as subject occur not alone through the medium of the state as the sovereign political authority and public sphere of government in society. They occur in virtually every other form of society as well, starting with the family. All established human groups and institutions have their inner structure of authority, their pattern of ruler-subject relations. If they stand outside the institutional structure of the state, they are not on that account nongovernmental. Rather, they belong to the sphere of private as distinguished from public government. Government itself, in the elementary sense of rulership of man over man, is pervasive in human society.

All this is more than ordinarily pertinent in an assessment of Marx as a political thinker. For perhaps more than any other important Western political theorist, either before his time or after, he was concerned with private government, particularly as expressed in the economic life of man in history. Indeed, private government in the economic life was for him the primary and decisive realm of the political, and public government—the sphere of the state—was a secondary and subordinate political field. Marx's economic interpretation of politics went along with a political interpretation of economics. If politics was "about economics," economics was political through and through.

This attribute of Marx's thought reflected the Hegelian heritage of the materialist conception of history, the influence of *The Phenomenology of Mind* in particular. His inversion of Hegel's political philosophy in the critical commentary of 1843 led him to the view that civil society underlay the state. But Marx did not for long visualize this civil society in the manner of the classical political economists, for whom it was a society of free, self-interested economic men interacting as equals in the marketplace. The image of it underwent a profound transformation in his mind, as shown by his original formulation of the materialist conception of history in the Paris manuscripts of 1844. There the "economic men" in civil society reduced themselves to two archetypal figures: the worker and the capitalist. And in conceptualizing the relation between them, Marx was guided by the section of the *Phenomenology* in which Hegel had depicted the dualization of spirit into "Master and Servant" (*"Herr und Knecht"*). This was shown by the terminology he employed. He spoke of the capitalist as *"Herr,"* the worker as *"Knecht,"* and the labor itself as a condition of *"Knechtschaft,"* or bondage. The fundamental socioeconomic relationship in civil society was thus politicized. The capital-labor relation became, in Marx's mind, a "politicoeconomic" relation of dominion and servitude, and always remained that. Indeed, this is one of the significant expressions of the underlying continuity in Marx's thought from the 1844 manuscripts to *Capital*.

Not only capitalism but every previous socioeconomic order founded on division of labor came to be viewed as a realm of the political. The "social relations of production," which had formed the foundation of society in every historical epoch, were relations not simply of economic exploitation but also of domination and servitude; the pervasive form of government in history was private government in the society of production. And this followed logically from Marx's basic premises as analyzed earlier. Since each historical form of the division of labor in production had been a form of captivity for the producers, the domination of man by man was necessarily involved in the very process of production. So, for Marx, man as possessor of the means of production was *ruler* over man as producer. He was so not simply as the force controlling the public government in the given society. His dominion over the producer was manifested first of all in economic life itself. It was precisely as owners—of slaves in ancient society, land in feudal society, and capital in bourgeois society—that men of one class tyrannized over men of another. Not surprisingly, then, Marx saw the quest for wealth and property as a kind of will to power. The capitalist profit motive, in particular, was a politico-economic drive for power over men through the possession of money. "Accumulation is a conquest of the world of social wealth," wrote Marx. "It increases the mass of human material exploited by the capitalist, and thus amplifies his direct and indirect dominion (*Herrschaft*)." A footnote to this passage commented: "In his study of the usurer, the old-fashioned but perennially renewed form of the capitalist, Luther shows forcibly that the love of power is an element in the impulse to acquire wealth."[44] Thus the capitalist "economic man" was for Marx a special kind of *homo politicus*, and avarice, the ruling passion of capitalist society, was seen as a passion to conquer and dominate human beings, to rule over them in the process of exploiting their labor.

Adumbrated already in the 1844 manuscripts, Marx's political interpretation of capitalist economics received its fullest and clearest expression in *Capital*. This book, which must be seen as his chief treatise of political theory as well as economics, is a vast elaboration of his original picture of the relationship between capitalist and worker as *Herr* and

44. *Capital*, p. 651.

Knecht. Although legally free to seek employment where he will and terminate it when he will, the worker is compelled by the necessity of earning a living for himself and his family to enter a relationship of servitude to the employer, a condition of "wage slavery." The language that Marx uses in portraying this capital-labor relation is replete with political terminology. In *Capital* he variously describes it as a "dictatorship of capital," "autocracy of capital," and "despotism of capital." The capitalist economic order appears here as a supremely authoritarian private realm of the political. It is a special form of command economy where the capitalist qua capitalist acts as a tyrannical ruling authority comparable to the great oriental despots of antiquity:

> The power that used to be concentrated in the hands of Asiatic or Egyptian kings or of Etruscan theocrats and the like, has in modern society been transferred to the capitalists—it may be to individual capitalists; or it may be to collective capitalists, as in joint-stock companies.[45]

The despotism of capital is decentralized. The politicalized command economy is enclosed within the confines of the productive unit, which in modern society is the factory. Marx sees the capitalists ruling over men and their productive activity in the factories rather as feudal lords once ruled over serfs on their estates. He repeatedly likens the private government inside the factory to a military dictatorship, where "The command of the capitalist in the field of production has become no less indispensable than the command of the general in the battlefield."[46] We read in the *Communist Manifesto* that

45. *Ibid.,* p. 350.
46. *Ibid.,* p. 346.

Masses of laborers, crowded into the factory, are organized like soldiers. As privates of the industrial army they are placed under the command of a perfect hierarchy of officers and sergeants. Not only are they slaves of the bourgeois class, and of the bourgeois state; they are daily and hourly enslaved by the machine, by the over-looker, and, above all, by the individual bourgeois manufacturer himself.

The same theme repeatedly recurs in *Capital*. Here again Marx describes the workers and overseers as "the private soldiers and non-commissioned officers of an industrial army." And, speaking of the factory code, he says that in it

capital formulates its autocracy over its workers—in a private legislative system, and without the partition of authority and the representative methods which in other fields are so much loved by the bourgeoisie. . . . In place of the slave driver's lash, we have the overseer's book of penalties.[47]

Because he devoted relatively very little space in his voluminous writings to general discussion of the state, it is easy to infer that Marx was only secondarily a political thinker. But such a view would be a superficial one. His major work, *Capital*, was in its special way a study in rulership. Its central theme was as much political as economic. It was the theme of tyranny in modern man's life of production, and of an inevitable final revolt by the worker-subjects against the "despotism of capital." Marx's economics of capitalism was quite literally a "political economy"—the phrase that he himself always used in referring to economics. To analyze it in these terms is to see Marx as the essentially political thinker that he was. His vision of the political saw

47. *Ibid.*, p. 452.

the productive process itself as the prime field of power relations between man and man. And his position as a political philosopher was basically determined by this vision.

The Anarchism of Marx

The central problem in the modern history of political philosophy in the West has been that of legitimizing state power, of specifying the conditions under which the sovereign ruling authority in society can be considered a rightful authority. Political theorists have addressed themselves to the basic question: What requirements must the sovereign state meet in order to be adjudged a good state? Their diverse answers have generally been predicated upon the assumption that the state derives its legitimacy from fulfilling such universal needs of the citizens as the needs for security and liberty.

In these terms Marx both was and was not a political philosopher. On the one hand, he never addressed himself to the problem of legitimizing state power. But on the other hand, he did have a definite position with regard to this problem. He had a normative as well as descriptive theory of the state. Stated very simply and briefly, it held that there are *no* conditions under which the state can be adjudged a good state. Marx believed that the sovereign political authority in society could not under any circumstances be considered a rightful authority. The state qua state was evil. Every historical example of the state, whether in the past, present or future, would inevitably partake of this evil. Accordingly, Marx's normative position with regard to the state was anarchism, which may be defined as the view that state power, being evil in essence, cannot possibly be legitimized.

This formulation of Marx's political philosophy may seem contradicted by his attitude toward the proletarian dictatorship that he believed to be historically imminent. Did he not devoutly desire the coming of this dictatorship? Must he not, then, have believed it to be something good? The answer to the first question is quite clearly affirmative, but does not imply an affirmative answer to the second. Marx, as we have already seen, did not hold the proletarian political order to be a good or a just one; he considered it at best a necessary evil on the road of man's entry into a higher form of society which would be a good society and as such stateless. The proletarian dictatorship was only a way station to something beyond and something different: society without a state. As a means to this end, it was desirable; as a form of state, it was not. As a state the proletarian state would doubtless be less evil than any other in history, but an evil it would be.

Marx's anarchism, like that of other political philosophers who have embraced the anarchist position, was grounded in a philosophical affirmation of freedom as the supreme human value and a belief that the existence of the state is incompatible with the realization of freedom. "Free state— what is this?" he caustically inquired in commenting on the draft Gotha Program's statement that the German workers' party aimed to create "the free state."[48] Freedom and the state, as he saw it, were mutually exclusive concepts. Insofar as any state existed, man would remain unfree; and liberated man would enjoy not freedom *in* the state but freedom *from* it. Mankind's leap from the kingdom of necessity to the kingdom of freedom would take place only with the advent of the higher phase of communist society. Certain functions of public administration and direction of the processes of production would still remain at that phase. They would not be performed, however, by a state in Marx's def-

48. Marx and Engels, *Selected Works*, II, 29.

inition of the term ("a special organism separated from society through the division of labor"). To underline this point, Engels, in his letter to the party leader August Bebel on the Gotha Program, suggested on behalf of himself and Marx that the word "state" be deleted from the statement of the party's goals: "We would therefore propose to replace 'state' everywhere by 'community' (*Gemeinwesen*), a good old German word which can very well represent the French word '*commune*'."[49]

A final problem emerges with the recognition that classical Marxism is committed to an anarchist position in its political philosophy. For if we consider Anarchism not as an abstract political philosophy but as a revolutionary movement associated with a political philosophy,[50] then we are confronted with the fact that Marxism was deeply at odds with it. Marxism and Anarchism were rival strains in European left-wing radicalism in the middle and later years of the nineteenth century. The rivalry originated at the time of Marx's break with Proudhon in the 1840's. It later found expression in the bitter feud between Marx and the Russian Anarchist Michael Bakunin, and their respective followers. The depth of the resulting division in European socialism was mirrored in Marx's reaction to the outbreak of the Franco-Prussian War of 1870. "The French need a thrashing," he wrote to Engels, explaining that a Prussian victory would foster a transfer of the center of gravity of the Western European workers' movement from France to Germany, which "would also mean the predominance of our theory over Proudhon's, etc."[51]

If we assume, as I believe we must, that the rivalry between Marxism and Anarchism was grounded in serious theoretical as well as personal differences between their

49. *Selected Correspondence*, p. 337.
50. To express this distinction, I here capitalize the word when referring to the movement but not when referring to the abstract philosophy.
51. *Selected Correspondence*, p. 292.

leaders, the theoretical differences require explanation. How is it that classical Marxism, while embracing anarchism as a political philosophy, disagreed with Anarchism as a socialist ideology? The question has generally been answered by reference to an extremely serious difference over the strategy of transition to a stateless society. The Anarchists did not propose to create a workers' state in the revolutionary process of leading humanity to a stateless future. Instead, they viewed the dismantling of statehood as part and parcel of the revolutionary process. The workers' revolution itself was to be antistatist. Commenting on this position, Engels wrote:

> The Anarchists put the thing upside down. They declare that the proletarian revolution must *begin* by doing away with the political organization of the state. . . . But to destroy it at such a moment would be to destroy the only organism by means of which the victorious proletariat can assert its newly-conquered power, hold down its capitalist adversaries, and carry out that economic revolution of society without which the whole victory must end in a new defeat and in a mass slaughter of the workers similar to those after the Paris Commune.[52]

The two doctrines were thus at odds over the issue of whether a state was needed for the purpose of abolishing the state. As Lenin later put it on behalf of the Marxists,

---

52. Letter to Van Patten of April 18, 1883, *Selected Correspondence*, p. 417. The Commune naturally caused intense controversy between the rival movements. The Anarchists saw the Paris insurrection as an antistatist revolution, and on this account Bakunin accused the Marxists of betraying their principles in claiming that the program and the aim of the Commune were theirs. They contended, on the other hand, that the Commune was the first historical incarnation of the dictatorship of the proletariat.

We do not at all disagree with the Anarchists on the question of the abolition of the state as an aim. We maintain that, to achieve this aim, we must temporarily make use of the instruments, resources, and methods of the state power against the exploiters. . . .[53]

But a deeper theoretical cleavage underlay this significant strategic difference. Anarchism did more than declare the state qua state to be evil; it also singled out the state as the principal evil in society, the decisive cause and expression of human unfreedom. For reasons dealt with earlier here, classical Marxism rejected such a view. Although it was anarchist in treating the state qua state as evil, it was opposed to the Anarchist doctrine on the state as the prime locus of evil. It saw man's unfreedom in the state as something secondary to, and derivative from, his unfreedom in the polity of production. The decisive cause and principal form of human bondage, and thus the supreme evil in history, was not subjection to the state but the imprisonment of man within the division of labor in production. The supreme end, therefore, was the "economic emancipation of labor" via the overthrow of the relations of domination and servitude in economic life. The emancipation of man from the state would follow as a matter of course.

We have direct testimony from Engels showing that this was his and Marx's understanding of the opposition between Marxism and Anarchism. Bakunin's position, he said in a letter of January 24, 1872 to Theodor Cuno, was that capital existed by courtesy of the state, which was therefore the main evil to be abolished.

As, therefore, the state is the chief evil, it is above all the state which must be done away with and then capitalism will go to hell of itself. We, on the contrary say:

53. *The State and Revolution*, in V. I. Lenin, *Selected Works*, II, 181. For a similar view, see Plamenatz, *Man and Society*, II, 374, 383.

do away with capital, the appropriation of the whole means of production in the hands of the few, and the state will fall away of itself. The difference is an essential one. Without a previous social revolution the abolition of the state is nonsense; the abolition of capital *is* in itself the social revolution and involves a change in the whole mode of production.[54]

The special anarchism of Marx and Engels must thus be seen as an anarchism directed primarily against authoritarianism in the society of production and only secondarily against authoritarianism as exemplified in the state. The tyranny from which it aimed to deliver man chiefly was that which he endured as a subject of the sovereign state of capital—the "despotism of capital."

What communism ultimately signified to Marx was man's complete and perfect freedom in the life of production. The revolutionary abolition of private property and therewith of the social division of labor between classes would lead, he thought, to the overcoming of the division of labor in all its subordinate forms. Men would no longer be bound down for life to a single form of activity; the slavery of specialization would thereby be overthrown. Even within the modern factory, the abolition of the capitalist mode of production—wage labor—would bring emancipation of the worker from bondage to a particular form of specialized work. The shortening of the working day would give him leisure, and rotation of jobs within the factory would free him from the tyranny of specialization in what remained of factory work. The economic life-process of society would be carried on by "a free association of producers,"[55] undivided into *Herr* and *Knecht*.

In his short essay of 1872 "On Authority," which was written against the Anarchists, Engels implicitly contra-

54. *Selected Correspondence*, pp. 319–320.
55. *Capital*, p. 54.

dicted Marx's vision of the factory of the future as a realm of freedom in the life of production. "The automatic machinery of a big factory is much more despotic than the small capitalists who employ workers have ever been," he wrote. "Wanting to abolish authority in large-scale industry is tantamount to wanting to abolish industry itself, to destroy the power loom in order to return to the spinning wheel."[56] Yet a nonauthoritarian existence in the factory was integral to communism itself in Marx's understanding of it, and this was a central message of his political philosophy.

56. Marx and Engels, *Selected Works*, II, p. 637.

Chapter Four

MARXISM AND MODERNIZATION

◇◇◇◇◇◇◇◇◇◇◇◇◇◇◇◇◇◇◇◇◇◇◇◇◇◇◇◇◇◇◇◇

Since the Second World War, the social sciences have shown a pronounced tendency to become developmental. Such influential titles as *The Passing of Traditional Society*, *The Stages of Economic Growth*, and *The Politics of Developing Areas* reflect the effort to build change, growth, and development into our conception of society. In this connection, the archetypal triad "ancient–medieval–modern," a way of thinking about the history of Western society, has tended to give way to "traditional–transitional–modern"—an attempt to conceptualize *all* societies in developmental terms. In short, modernization has become a dominant concern of contemporary social science. History, economics, political science, sociology, and psychology appear to be converging upon a theory of modernization as one of the central structures of our thinking about man and society.

Here lies one of the explanations for the recent renaissance of interest in Marxism. It helps to explain, too, the increasing concern with the "appeals of Marxism," which might be described as the problem of what it is that has made Marxism historically important irrespective of whether or not it is scientifically true. The reason why the quest for a theory of modernization has contributed to the revival of interest in Marxism is easily stated. When social scientists embarked upon this quest in the mid-twentieth century, they found that Marx and Engels had preceded them by a century or more. Although the term "modernization" does not appear in their writings, the *theme* frequently does. Not only did Marx and Engels propound a general theory of society that was developmental in essence; they dealt in many places with the problems of the emergence of modern society. Was not volume one of *Capital* a study and theory of the transformation of "feudal" (i.e., traditional) into "bourgeois" (i.e., modern) society? Can we not view Marx's reflections on peasant society in *The Eighteenth Brumaire of Louis Bonaparte* as a contribution to the analysis of traditional society in general?[1] What were his articles on British rule in India if not a commentary on the process of modernization in a typical "underdeveloped" country? And may not the *Communist Manifesto* be seen as, among other things, a manifesto of modernization-theory? Such, for example, is the view taken by W. W. Rostow, who subtitled *The Stages of Economic Growth* "A Non-Communist Manifesto" and presented his theory of modernization in critical counterpoint to Marx's. Indeed, his book's clearly expressed aim was to improve upon and supersede the theory of modernization implicit in the 1848 *Manifesto* of Marx and Engels. Here we may pause to reflect that it is no common thing in the modern era for an

---

1. See, for example, chapter 2, "Marx, Modernity, and Mobilization," in Lloyd I. Rudolph and Susanne Hoeber Rudolph, *The Modernization of Tradition: Political Development in India* (Chicago and London: The University of Chicago Press, 1967).

intellectual construction to stand for 112 years as a regnant position in its field. And whether the contemporary theorists of modernization have yet displaced the Marxist view is open to question. Certainly it has not yet received the all-round critical assessment that it merits.

There is no denying the importance of Marx and Engels as forerunners and exponents of the theory of modernization. On the other hand, we should not make the mistake of seeing them only as such. I cannot agree with Rostow, for example, when he writes that "in its essence" Marxism is

a theory of how traditional societies come to build compound interest into their structures by learning the tricks of modern industrial technology; and of the stages that will follow until they reach that ultimate stage of affluence which, in Marx's view, was not Socialism, under the dictatorship of the proletariat, but true Communism.[2]

For Marxism, as has been shown in the foregoing chapters, is far more than this. Its subject is man as a species. In essence it is a theory of mankind's historical growth process and final self-realization in a post-historical society that Marx treats under the heading of "socialism" or "communism." Moreover, the classical Marxist writings do not deal with future socialism and communism in relation to the process of modernization. Rather, as will be discussed in greater detail below, they picture this process as one that fully unfolds during the bourgeois social epoch and belongs to future communist society only as its inheritance. Ac-

2. *The Stages of Economic Growth: A Non-Communist Manifesto* (Cambridge: The Cambridge University Press, 1960), p. 45. A somewhat similar view is suggested by Adam Ulam when he writes that "Marxism is *about* industrialism," in *The Unfinished Revolution: An Essay on the Sources of Influence of Marxism and Communism* (New York: Random House, 1960), p. 60.

cordingly, it was left to Marxism in its later Leninist extension to devolop the theory as well as the practice of communism as a modernizing society.

The Process of Modernization

But if classical Marxism is not simply a theory of modernization, it does contain one, at least implicitly. Its treatment of the emergence of modern society out of feudalism presents a Marxist "model" of the modernization process. According to this model, modernization is essentially a process of the rise of capitalist enterprise, with a multitude of consequences affecting every aspect of society and human consciousness. In the well-known Chapter 24 of *Capital*, Marx traced the process to its origin in so-called "primary accumulation." This was the decomposition of feudal society under pressure of a series of developments that resulted in the divorce of the producer from the means of production: the abolition of serfdom, the liberation of the town workers from the restrictions of the medieval guilds, the expropriation of the agricultural population through the enclosures, and the emergence of the industrial capitalist. The prehistory of capitalism in England was taken as the typical form of "primary accumulation."

For Marx, then, the agrarian feudal society of the medieval West, dominated by the class division between serf labor and the landowning nobility, was the general prototype of traditional society in its immediate premodern form. Modernization was the social transformation engendered by the rise and spread of the capitalist mode of production, as it occurred in post-medieval Western Europe. An economic revolution, the change from serf labor to wage labor as the dominant mode of productive activity, was the precondition of it. Further, the process of modernization was not only economically generated but economically governed in its subsequent development; its driving force was the capitalists' urge to aggrandize their capital by exploitation of proletarian wage labor in the factory, and their derivative drive to modernize the technological processes of production as one of the means of capital accumulation.

What about the role of politics in the classical Marxist model? While it would not be precisely true to say that for Marx and Engels there was no "politics of modernization," it could be said that they did not see politics as a fulcrum of the process, or a political revolution as its *sine qua non*. True, the development of capitalist society necessitated at some point a political revolution to displace the old monarchical regime and bring the bourgeois class to power in what Marx and Engels called the "modern representative state"—the classic case being the French Revolution. But such a political struggle and upheaval was not required in order to give the process of modernization its motive power and momentum. These latter were imminent in the process of capitalist economic enterprise itself, its developmental dynamics, its inner dialectic. It was only when the old feudal forms and relations turned into an obstacle to the full and free development of the productive powers of capital that politics became vital to the process of modernization. At that point, the rising capitalist class was impelled to clear away the obstacles by conquering state power and converting the government into its own instrumentality, "a committee for managing the common affairs of the whole bourgeoisie."[3]

---

3. *The Communist Manifesto,* in Marx and Engels, *Selected Works,* I, 36. This should be qualified by the reminder that Marx and Engels saw the bourgeoisie as gradually increasing its political influence in society during the long period preceding its revolutionary conquest of power. On this, see *ibid.,* pp. 35–36.

Modernization, according to the classical Marxist model, is a process that has an agent, a class in society acting as its spearhead and expediter, and this class is the bourgeoisie. The peasants and artisans are its victims; the capitalists are its champions. This may explain the rapturous passages in the *Communist Manifesto* that sing the deeds of the bourgeoisie:

> It has been the first to show what man's activity can bring about. It has accomplished wonders far surpassing Egyptian pyramids, Roman aqueducts, and Gothic cathedrals; it has conducted expeditions that put in the shade all former Exoduses of nations and crusades.

Driven by the imperatives of technological development and commercial-industrial expansion that, in Marx's view, are inherent in capitalist enterprise as a competitive struggle, the bourgeoisie implants the capitalist mode of production far and wide, creates a world market, urbanizes society, and subjects the countryside to the rule of the towns. It agglomerates the means of production, concentrates property in a few hands, develops the administratively centralized nation-state with its uniform code of laws and national class-interest. In a word, it modernizes society:

> The bourgeoisie, during its rule of scarce one hundred years, has created more massive and more colossal productive forces than have all preceding generations together. Subjection of nature's forces to man, machinery, application of chemistry to industry and agriculture, steam-navigation, railways, electric telegraphs, clearing of whole continents for cultivation, canalization of rivers, whole populations conjured out of the ground—what earlier century had even a presentiment

that such productive forces slumbered in the lap of social labor?[4]

Marx's positive attitude toward the rising bourgeoisie was understandable. Being revolutionary through and through, he could not help admiring the bourgeoisie in its historical role as a revolutionary class. For this was how he saw it. "The bourgeoisie cannot exist without constantly revolutionizing the instruments of production, and thereby the relations of production, and with them the whole relations of society," he wrote in the *Manifesto*.

> Constant revolutionizing of production, uninterrupted disturbance of all social conditions, everlasting uncertainty and agitation, distinguish the bourgeois epoch from all earlier ones. All fixed, fast-frozen relations, with their train of ancient and venerable prejudices and opinions, are swept away, all new-formed ones become antiquated before they can ossify.

Goaded by the thirst for profit and coerced by the need to innovate as the prerequisite of survival in the competitive war of all against all, the capitalists were continually transforming the methods and relations of production. The permanent revolution in the economic base was churning up the institutions, forms of community, life styles, culture, ideas, and values handed down from the past—all that belonged to the social superstructure. This bourgeois socio-economic revolution was Marx's image of modernization.

He saw it not only as a complete transformation of society on a national scale, but as an international phenomenon. Although initiated in Western Europe, the capitalist revolution of modernization was world-wide in scope and effect. At the beginning it had gained momentum from the discovery and colonization of America, the rounding of the

4. *Ibid.*, pp. 38–39.

Cape, and the development of the East Indian and Chinese markets. With the development of modern machine industry, the ever-expanding markets grew into a world market, which in turn stimulated the further expansion of industry, commerce, navigation, and railways. And so the bourgeois revolution turned into a world revolution:

> The bourgeoisie . . . draws all, even the most barbarian, nations into civilization. The cheap prices of its commodities are the heavy artillery with which it batters down all Chinese walls, with which it forces the barbarians' intensely obstinate hatred of foreigners to capitulate. It compels all nations, on pain of extinction, to adopt the bourgeois mode of production; it compels them to introduce what it calls civilization into their midst, i.e., to become bourgeois themselves. In one word, it creates a world after its own image.[5]

Modernization was thus seen as a universal process starting in Europe and eventually comprising the modernization of the whole world through the diffusion of bourgeois civilization to the backward countries. In two articles published in *The New York Daily Tribune* in 1853, Marx looked at India from this point of view. India's heritage of backwardness was connected, on the one hand, with the Asiatic mode of production, under which the government provides the public works required for artificial irrigation of vast territories on a low level of civilization; and, on the other, with the age-old village community living its semi-independent life of agricultural pursuits combined with domestic industry. British rule, by uprooting the cottage industry, by blowing up the economic base of the Indian village system, was causing the only *social* revolution ever heard of in Asia. Noting that the atomized village commu-

5. *Ibid.,* p. 38.

nities had been the foundation of Oriental despotism, that they were contaminated by distinctions of caste and by slavery, that they "subjugated man to external circumstances instead of elevating man to be the sovereign of circumstances," Marx said that England, no matter how vile her motives and how great her crimes in India, was the unconscious tool of history in bringing about such a fundamental revolution in the social state of Asia.[6] And in the second of his two articles, he returned to the theme of British imperialism's revolutionary role in India. By giving the country an administrative and political unity based upon modern communications, organizing a native army along modern lines, introducing a free press, training a native ruling class imbued with European science, building a railway system and other prerequisites for Indian industrialization, ruining the native industry, and undermining the village community as the unit of Indian life, England was fulfilling a double mission. On the one hand it was destroying the old Asiatic society; on the other it was laying the material foundations of Western society in Asia.[7] The revolution of modernization, led by the bourgeoisie in Europe, was being brought to Asia by European imperialism as a revolution of Westernization.

Meanwhile, the process of modernization had entered upon a new stage in the advanced countries of Europe and in America, the stage of capitalist decline. Capitalism, which had emerged as a corrosive force for change, was no longer that. The bourgeoisie, which had risen to the leadership and

---

6. "The British Rule in India," in Marx and Engels, *Selected Works*, I, 350–351.

7. "The Future Results of British Rule in India," in *Selected Works*, I, 353–356. In another revealing passage of this article, Marx wrote: "The day is not far distant when, by a combination of railways and steam vessels, the distance between England and India, measured by time, will be shortened to eight days, and when that once fabulous country will thus be actually annexed to the Western world."

command of society as the agent of a revolutionary transformation of traditional society, had now turned into a
deeply conservative class, albeit one that was being driven
by self-seeking motives to export the revolution of modernization to the colonial world. True, the production processes themselves remained a sphere of permanent revolution owing to the harsh necessity of competitive innovation.
Even under mature capitalism, therefore, the technological
base continued to expand and develop, making possible, for
the first time in history, a society of material abundance for
all. But the productive potential of modern machine industry could not be realized on the basis of the existing relations of production between capital and labor. That these
relations had become a "fetter" upon the productive powers
was shown by the commercial crises of overproduction that
periodically convulsed bourgeois society. In an Afterword
to the second German edition of *Capital*, published in 1873,
Marx forecast that these crises would reach their crowning
point in an impending "universal crisis" that was already in
its preliminary stage.[8]

In this advanced phase of development, according to
Marx and Engels, bourgeois society becomes both more and
more modernized and more and more deeply deranged as
the class struggle develops between bourgeoisie and proletariat. The means of production are increasingly concentrated and the labor processes become more cooperative or
"socialized" in character as well as more mechanized. At the
same time, the system of capitalist production grows more
and more cosmopolitan, and the nation-state becomes obsolete as the institutional framework of society. "National
differences and antagonisms between peoples are daily more
and more vanishing, owing to the development of the bourgeoisie, to freedom of commerce, to the world market, to

8. Marx and Engels, *Selected Works*, I, 457.

uniformity in the mode of production and in the conditions of life corresponding thereto," states the *Communist Manifesto*, adding: "The supremacy of the proletariat will cause them to vanish still faster."[9] But the emergent world society of the late bourgeois era is a polarized society engulfed in class war between the vast mass of proletarian wage workers and the small minority of capitalist magnates who have survived in the competitive struggle. The class war is destined to reach its peak in an open revolt of the workers against the dehumanization of life and labor to which capitalism condemns them. Marx and Engels expected the proletarian upheaval to break out in a number of leading countries and become the fulcrum of world revolution, since capitalism and the world market had transformed society into a global unit.

Modernization and Communism

As has been explained in the previous chapters, Marx and Engels distinguished between lower and higher phases of the universal communist society that would issue from the proletarian revolution. The lower phase, which Marx had called "raw communism" in his *Economic and Philosophical Manuscripts of 1844*, would be the regime of proletarian revolution itself—society under worker dictatorship on the morrow of the overthrow of the bourgeoisie and seizure and socialization of the means of production by the work-

9. *Ibid.*, p. 51. Elsewhere in the *Manifesto*, they write: "In place of the old local and national seclusion and self-sufficiency, we have intercourse in every direction, universal interdependence of nations. . . . National one-sidedness and narrow-mindedness become more and more impossible, and from the numerous national and local literatures, there arises a world literature" (*ibid.*, p. 38). See also Marx's statement in *Capital* (p. 846) that "All the peoples of the world are enmeshed in the net of the world market and therefore the capitalist regime tends more and more to assume an international character."

ing class. Capitalism—the exploitation of wage labor for the accumulation of capital—would now have been supplanted by production for social needs. But given the technical problems of transition and the survival of habits and attitudes bred under the old social order, it would temporarily be necessary to remunerate people according to the amount of labor performed. In the ensuing higher phase of communist society, the productive powers created under capitalism and liberated by the proletarian revolution would provide sufficient goods for distribution to take place according to need; and fully humanized individuals would seek diverse forms of productive activity no longer under the spur of necessity, as always in the past, but as avenues for spontaneous self-expression.

Contrary to the suggestion of W. W. Rostow that Marx's lower and higher phases of communist society correspond to the stages of "maturity" and "high mass-consumption" in his own stages-of-economic-growth analysis of modernization,[10] Marx did not basically conceive of socialism or communism in terms of economic growth. It is true, as just indicated, that he distinguished lower and higher stages of communist society, and envisaged full economic abundance only in the higher phase. But the advance from the lower to the higher stage would not involve industrialization or similar long-range economic developmental processes. For the world that the workers were destined to win by revolution would already be highly industrialized, particularly in the advanced countries chiefly in question. The proletarians would thus inherit a world ripe for abundance.

The economic mission of the proletarian revolution would not be to *develop* the productive powers of society, but to *free* them from the "fetters" clamped upon them by

10. "As against our stages—the traditional society; the preconditions; take-off; maturity; and high mass-consumption—we are setting, then, Marx's feudalism; bourgeois capitalism; Socialism; and Communism" (*The Stages of Economic Growth*, p. 145).

the nature of capitalist economy. Untold possibilities of rapid growth of output were inherent in the discrepancy between the huge industrial potentiality created by capitalism and the actual economic performance of that system. As Engels put the point in an essay on Marx published in 1878, the productive powers created under the bourgeoisie

> are only waiting for the associated proletariat to take possession of them in order to bring about a state of things in which every member of society will be enabled to participate not only in production but also in the distribution and administration of social wealth, and which so increases the social productive forces and their yield by planned operation of the whole of production that the satisfaction of all reasonable needs will be assured to everyone in an ever-increasing measure.[11]

Inevitably, it would take some time, after the wresting of the means of production from the bourgeoisie, for the regime of proletarian revolution to organize production, administration, and distribution on the new basis; and it was largely on this account that Marx and Engels made provision in their scheme for the lower phase as a transitional period. But because of their view that society at the time of the revolution would be materially quite ripe for reconstruction along communist lines, they did not imagine that the transitional period would be long as historical time is reckoned; a period of months or years rather than of decades seems to be what they envisaged.

Nor, on their assumptions, would it take a long time to alter the old work habits and attitudes characteristic of bourgeois society. Contrary to what many have supposed, Marx and Engels had a very high—perhaps too high—view

11. Marx and Engels, *Selected Works*, II, 151. It must also be considered that Marx and Engels had a far more modest and limited conception of the meaning of "all reasonable needs" than might a present-day citizen of a consumption-oriented society.

of human nature. Growing out of their intellectual sources in German philosophy from Hegel to Feuerbach, this view pictured man as in essence a "free conscious producer," as Marx expressed it in the 1844 manuscripts: a consciously, spontaneously productive animal with an innate flair for artistic creation, even in his material producing activity, and for aesthetic enjoyment of the world of created objects. In the course of history, therefore, man had not been a fully human being; he had been "alienated man." As economic man (not Marx's phrase) in historical forms of class society—for example, as the avaricious capitalist of the bourgeois period or the proletarian concerned only with making enough to keep himself and family alive—man was estranged from his human nature. But once the social relations that kept him in this unnatural condition were radically changed, a correspondingly radical change would soon take place in him owing to the assertion of his human tendencies. Once the urge of a minority to accumulate capital *ad infinitum* had ceased to be the driving force of production, the life of the vast majority would cease to be a mere struggle for subsistence. At this point—the point of the revolution—man could finally begin leading a fully human productive life, which meant not only a freely productive one but also one of association, of community—in other words, of socialism or communism. Since it was man's nature to produce freely and in association, the transitional regime of proletarian revolution should not be a long-lived one. Its essential function was not to remold man by a long process of training into a new kind of being, but simply to liberate him to become for the first time himself, realizing the human potentialities that had always been suppressed during history.

As for the higher phase of communist society that lay beyond the transitional period, Marx did not conceive it as essentially a society of "high mass-consumption." Communism did not mean to Marx and Engels an "ultimate stage of affluence," although they imagined that there would be enough goods to satisfy "all reasonable needs." A definition of communism in terms of "high mass-consumption" would have evoked from Marx the same scorn and contempt that he showed for Benthamite utilitarianism and all philosophies that pictured man as essentially a pleasure-seeking animal.[12] Man being, in his view, a producer by nature, every form of society, including the ultimate post-historical one, was defined by its mode of productive activity. Communism was a form of society in which productive activity would cease to be labor and the old enslaving divisions of labor would be overcome. The fact that it would also be a society of abundance was important but secondary: important because man could not devote himself to productive pursuits in full freedom if he had to worry about material needs, secondary because the satisfaction of these needs was no more than a precondition of reaching the goal of history, not the goal itself.

Thus, at the projected future point of world proletarian revolution, the classical Marxist theory of history ceases to be a theory of modernization. For Marx and Engels, this future revolution would be the great break between the entire foregoing historical process of human development and a post-historical society that would be *beyond modernization*. Industrialization, urbanization, machine technology, the conquest of nature, the breakdown of traditional society in the backward countries, and the internationalization of society were all the work of the bourgeois era. The bourgeois revolution of modernization was the preparation of society for communism. The mission of the communist revolution was not to modernize society further, but to humanize it, to reintegrate man with himself and nature and make him, collectively, the "sovereign of circumstances."

12. For Marx's view of hedonism and utilitarianism, see *Philosophy and Myth in Karl Marx*, pp. 16–18.

At this point, further change itself would become civilized for the first time:

> When a great social revolution shall have mastered the results of the bourgeois epoch, the market of the world, and the modern powers of production, and subjected them to the common control of the most advanced peoples, then only will human progress cease to resemble that hideous pagan idol, who would not drink the nectar but from the skulls of the slain.[13]

Marx's conception of ultimate communism was consummatory. Beyond the vicissitudes of history lay a society of human self-realization in productive activities. Change, progress, and development were not excluded from this vision of the human future; but neither were they defining features of it. Superficial appearances to the contrary, Marx did not share that Victorian mystique of perpetual progress which inspired Tennyson—upon seeing the locomotive on display at the great London exposition—to write: "Let the great world spin forever down the ringing grooves of change." He too was inspired by the same sight, but what he wrote was: "Revolutions are the locomotives of history." Man's fate was not to go on traveling forever, but to proceed by revolutions to a final destination, an existential society. Such was Marx's orientation as a mind steeped in the Greek heritage, in German philosophy, and in nineteenth-century European socialism.

Strengths and Weaknesses of the Theory

Until recently, critical discussion of Marx's theory of bourgeois society has turned very largely upon his analysis of

13. "The Future Results of British Rule in India," in Marx and Engels, *Selected Works*, I, 358.

capitalism's inevitable decline and fall. Eduard Bernstein raised many of the key issues at the turn of the century in his revisionist critique of Marxism from within.[14] Some of the serious defects of classical Marxism's view of advanced capitalism were already evident. The observable tendencies of economic and social development in countries like England, France, and Germany were not all in line with the prospectus offered in the *Communist Manifesto, Capital,* and other basic writings of Marx and Engels. Commercial crises of overproduction were not going from bad to worse, and the predicted "universal crisis" had not arrived. Bourgeois societies in their maturity were not becoming more and more polarized between a small minority of immensely wealthy capitalist magnates on the one hand and a vast majority of increasingly miserable proletarians on the other. On the contrary, wealth was becoming more widely distributed, intermediate socioeconomic groups were holding their own or expanding, and industrial labor was winning improved working and living conditions. Consequently, modern society was not obeying the "economic law of motion" which Marx declared it his purpose to lay bare in *Capital:* it was not being propelled by the developmental dynamics of capitalism to revolutionary breakdown. Instead of turning into an arena of irreconcilable class war, bourgeois society was reforming itself through trade unionism and the political institutions of parliamentary democracy, and becoming *less* divided in the process.

But from the standpoint of the problem of modernization, what is most important in Marx is not his theory of the decline and fall of capitalism. Rather, it is his account of the rise and early development of bourgeois society. Only in the recent past, as interest had developed in creating a theory of modernization, has this aspect of Marx's thought

14. *Evolutionary Socialism* (New York: Schocken Books, 1961).

begun to be considered in its own terms and critically appraised. But perhaps because the theory of modernization is
not yet fully developed, we still lack an adequate critique
of Marx's position.

Viewed from the present vantage-point in time, a little
over a century after the publication of *Capital*, it shows
notable strengths as well as weaknesses. One of the strengths
is Marx's understanding that modernization is a revolutionary process, that it involves a total transformation of institutions, social, political, and legal as well as economic structures, life-styles, cultural values, and forms of consciousness.
Another is the perception that the transition to modernity,
like any other pervasive change in the pattern of human
living, normally involves intense conflict between social
forces in favor of the change and those opposing it. Still a
further strong point of Marx as a theorist of modernization
is his appreciation of the role of economic and technological
factors in the process. For here if anywhere the general
Marxist emphasis upon the primacy of economics has merit.
Even here, however, economic determinism needs to be
qualified for reasons to be discussed below.

On the other side of the balance-sheet, Marx's treatment
of modernization suffers from failure to take account of the
variability of the process. There are diverse patterns of modernization, and an adequate theory must reflect this fact in
its conceptual structure, as Marx's does not; it must be a
comparative theory. Working with a unilinear conception
of the world-historical process, and the notion of a particular socioeconomic formation as typical of each successive
epoch, Marx understands modernization under the aspect of
bourgeoisification only, and he takes the British case as generally illustrative of it. England was the "classic ground"
of modern capitalist development, he declared in the preface to the first German edition of *Capital*, considering the
possible objection that the model presented in the book

might not be applicable to Germany. And a study based largely upon British historical materials could confidently be taken as valid for other, less developed countries, since they, being subject to the same developmental laws, must necessarily evolve in the same way: "The country that is more developed industrially only shows, to the less developed, the image of its own future."[15]

But it was not to be so, at any rate in many instances. Even within the European setting, the second half of the nineteenth century witnessed considerable diversity, for example, in patterns of industrialization. Commenting on the statement of Marx just quoted, a present-day economic historian writes that while it contains a half-truth, "in several important respects the development of a backward country may, by the very virtue of its backwardness, tend to differ fundamentally from that of an advanced country."[16] Thus, not all European countries experienced a sudden spurt of industrialization along with a concentration upon heavy-industry development, agricultural Denmark being a case in point. Nor did the process of capitalist development take place everywhere in Europe with the spontaneity and absence of organized direction that were principal features of Marx's British-based model. In some countries the organized direction was supplied by investment

15. Marx and Engels, *Selected Works*, I, 449. Engels commented in a note to the 1888 edition of the *Communist Manifesto* that he and Marx had taken England as their model of bourgeois economic development, and France as typical of modern political development (*ibid.*, p. 36 n.). For a present-day study that shows the necessity for a comparative approach in the theory of modernization, see Cyril E. Black, *The Dynamics of Modernization: A Study in Comparative History* (New York, Evanston, and London: Harper and Row, 1966) especially chapters 2 and 4.

16. Alexander Gerschenkron, *Economic Backwardness in Historical Perspective* (New York: Praeger, 1965), p. 7. Speaking of Marx's conception of "primary capitalist accumulation," Professor Gerschenkron states that modern research has indicated the need for revisions in it, but that it "has a rather modern touch" and "testifies to the brilliance of Marx's intuition" (*ibid.*, pp. 34–36).

banks; in others, notably nineteenth-century Russia, it was supplied by the central state authority. Furthermore, historical experience showed in places the need for faith or ideology as a means of overcoming inertia. Hence the paradox of capitalist industrialization under the auspices of socialist ideologies, such as Saint-Simonism in nineteenth-century France.[17]

Against this it could be argued that industrialization is but one basic component of modernization, and that differences in the pace or mode of industrializing, such as those just instanced, are no more than incidental to the broader social process of transition to modernity. Whatever the specific differences in the pattern of capitalist development, whether there was a spurt-like industrialization or not, intervention by investment banks or not, etc., we still observe the emergence of modern bourgeois society. But this argument would hold good chiefly for Europe, particularly Western Europe, leaving Marx's paradigm open to the charge of Europocentrism. In conceiving modernization as the rise of capitalism and bourgeois society, he was generalizing European and North American historical experience into a universal process. From the perspective of the late twentieth century, we can easily see his error. Marx overestimated the potentialities of capitalism as an agency of the modernization of backward societies outside the Atlantic zone. He overestimated the historical role of the bourgeoisie, which in most non-Western societies did not become the powerful and corrosive force for modernizing change that it had been in Western Europe. There its modern role of leadership was prepared by the slow growth of experience of self-government in the setting of medieval cities. By virtue of its very

17. *Ibid.*, pp. 16–25, 44. As Professor Gerschenkron points out, "To break through the barriers of stagnation in a backward country, to ignite the imaginations of men, and to place their energies in the service of economic development, a stronger medicine is needed than the promise of better allocation of resources or even of the lower price of bread."

different historical experience, and of different socioeconomic conditions, the merchant class outside the West has generally lacked the qualifications to play a role similar to that of the Western bourgeoisie. So, in many parts of the world, modernization has not taken the form of bourgeoisification, nor has industrialization proceeded via the development of capitalism. Social forces other than the bourgeoisie have spearheaded modernization, and politics—specifically revolutionary politics—have been instrumental in giving the process its momentum.

Nonbourgeois Modernization

In looking more closely at this other form of the process, it may be useful to cast a critical glance at the concept of "transitional society." It is easy to assume that once a traditional society enters the passage to modernity, it is carried along under its own momentum to the destination, in other words, that a transitional society is a society actually *in transit*, at a slower or swifter pace, from traditionalism to a state of mature development describable as modernity. Such a roller coaster image of modernization misses, however, the real dynamics of the process, particularly in the setting of many non-Western societies. These dynamics are such that modernization proceeds by fits and starts. The society embarks upon modernization, but slows down in the process after a time and enters into a state of *arrested modernization*. Under a new impulse, often from above, i.e., from the government, it may make another push toward modernization, but only to bog down again after encountering formidable internal obstructions to further major change. Hence, a "transitional" society may not always be in the actual throes of modernizing change. Contrary to a euphemistic American usage, underdeveloped countries are not always "developing countries." They may, instead, be chronically underdeveloped, relatively stagnant, immobilized in mid-passage. Of course, change will not come to a complete stop. But if the obstructionist tendencies are strong enough to compete successfully with the modernizing tendencies, the processes of change may be slowed to such a creeping pace that the society is, broadly speaking, in a condition of stagnation.

Russia in the later eighteenth and first half of the nineteenth century provides a classic case of arrested modernization. In the seventeenth century, the Muscovite government had deliberately initiated a process of selective Westernization of Russian society. It did so out of a desire to take over techniques that would enable the huge but backward country to compete in power with its more advanced neighbors to the West. At the end of the seventeenth and beginning of the eighteenth century, Peter the Great forced the pace of events and transformed the process of selective borrowing and change into a veritable revolution from above, comprising industrialization, administrative reforms, educational development, forced Westernization of manners and dress, and so on. Under the impact of the Petrine revolution of modernization, Russian society took a long stride toward the modern European pattern. But the pace was not maintained, and in the later eighteenth century Russia settled into a sluggish condition of more or less arrested modernization—a condition that persisted through the long reign of "Iron Tsar" Nicholas I in the second quarter of the nineteenth century. The accession of his successor, Alexander II, in 1855 marked the beginning of a new push forward in Russia's modernization. Alexander sponsored the abolition of serfdom, and the emancipation decree of 1861 inaugurated a whole series of major modernizing reforms in the 1860's which gave new momentum to the long-stagnant process of Russia's Europeanization. These social, political, and administrative reforms provided both a setting and an impetus for the development of capitalist enterprise and further rapid industrialization of the country in the later nineteenth century. In certain respects, however, the process of modernization again slowed down in the latter part of the reign of Alexander II and under his more conservative successors; and the Russia that came under Bolshevik rule in the revolution of 1917 was still economically, socially, politically, and culturally an underdeveloped country.

What accounts for arrested modernization? As the case of Russia shows, we should beware of assuming that it is a shortage of natural resources, of the economic prerequisites of modernity, that causes the modernization process to subside at an incomplete stage, for there was no such shortage in Russia. We should look for the sources of arrested modernization in a limitation or failure of motivation for modernizing change, on the one hand, and in active resistances to it on the other. Thus the drive to modernize Russia in the seventeenth century and in Peter's time was essentially a governmental interest in acquiring the benefits of European material culture as a means of building Russian national power. "He sought in the West not civilization but technology," writes the historian Kliuchevsky of Peter the Great.[18] When the motivation for modernizing change is thus restricted, the attainment of the immediate ends in view may relieve the pressure behind the process. Furthermore, when the drive toward modernization is concentrated in the immensely dynamic personality of an autocratic leader like Peter, his passing from the scene may itself cause the drive to slacken.

But no account of arrested modernization can overlook the phenomenon of resistance. This may take the form of

18. V. O. Kliuchevsky, *Kurs russkoi istorii* (Moscow, 1937), IV, 21.

inertia, the hidebound opposition of a traditional mentality —among the peasantry, for example—to change of outlook, values, and ways of living. Alternatively and very importantly, resistance may come from a politically powerful upper class that enjoys a comfortable existence at the already attained level of modernization and fears that further extension of the process would undermine its material interest and style of life. Thus, in post-Petrine Russia the landowning nobility, which Peter had attempted to use as an instrument of Europeanization, gained the upper hand in the state, and "the drive to raise the productivity of national labor by means of European culture was transformed into intensified fiscal exploitation and police enslavement of the people itself."[19] In the ensuing era of Russia's arrested modernization, the landed aristocracy in its majority resisted the abolition of serfdom. Not until the initiative for change was taken again from above, by an autocratic monarch, was this institutional obstacle to Russia's further modernization finally removed, opening the way for the fresh spurt of national development in the 1860's.

In other countries, where the special Russian problem of eliminating serfdom has not existed, a landed aristocracy has impeded further modernizing change by its resistance to land reform and therewith to the development of the countryside; and this resistance has been all the more effective in the absence of a commercial middle class capable of playing the historical role of the Western bourgeoisie. Then too, the force responsible for arrested modernization may be imperialism. A colonial administration may, for example, assist and encourage the administrative and economic development of the country in its charge only up to a certain point, beyond which it strives to preserve the status quo by putting a brake on development. A similar situation may

19. *Ibid.*, p. 358.

come about in a formally independent country where foreign economic interests resist further modernizing change because they fear the potential impact of such change upon their position. Finally, it should be observed that the early phases of modernization normally create administrative and technical resources, such as roads, railways, and telegraph, which augment the capability of a change-resistant central authority to control the society under conditions short of a massive upheaval.[20]

A society of arrested modernization will typically present a picture also of *differential* modernization. Instead of more-or-less homogeneously undergoing partial change, as a test-tube solution may change color through and through with the addition of a new ingredient, such a society tends to divide into relatively modernized and relatively nonmodernized spheres. As a socioeconomic system it loses much of what homogeneity it still possessed in the traditional phase, becoming rather advanced in certain ways and remaining quite backward in others. To be sure, certain modern facilities, such as railways and telegraph, may cover the country as a whole, although without becoming fully accessible to the population as a whole. But the developmental process will essentially be very uneven. The large cities, and particularly the capital city, will become centers of concentrated economic development and affluence, with amenities comparable to those in highly advanced countries. These centers may be surrounded, however, by primitive urban

20. Writing in 1906, Trotsky said of Russia: "At the moment when developing bourgeois society began to see a need for the political institutions of the West, the autocracy proved to be armed with all the material might of the European states. It rested upon a centralized bureaucratic machine which was quite useless for establishing new relations but was able to develop great energy in carrying out systematic repressions. The enormous distances of the country had been overcome by the telegraph, which imparts confidence to the actions of the administration and gives uniformity and rapidity to its proceedings (in the matter of repressions). The railways render it possible to throw military forces rapidly from one end of the country to the other." *Permanent Revolution and Results and Prospects* (London: New Park Publications, 1962), p. 175.

slums, and the rural interior of the country may be scarcely touched by modernity save on large estates inhabited by the wealthy few.

Culturally, too, the society of arrested modernization tends to become bifurcated. A minority of the population belonging to the upper and middle classes acquires advanced education, often at foreign universities, while the peasant masses remain largely illiterate. The minority assimilates modern secularized culture, including ideas, values, manners, and styles of dress; the majority stays pretty much under the influence of the traditional culture and folkways. So great and visible may be the resulting cultural rift in the society that there appear to be two different nations inhabiting one country. Again the history of Russian society affords a classic example. There emerged in the eighteenth century an upper-class minority of Russians—government officials, landowners, and military officers for the most part —who were European in dress and manner, spoke European languages, spent parts of their lives in European countries, and in some cases studied in European universities. As writers in the following century often expressed it, there were "two Russias." Alexander Herzen wrote that the modernizing reform of Peter the Great, that "crowned revolutionary," divided Russia into two parts. One was the Europeanized upper-class minority; the other was "old Russia, conservative, traditional, strictly Orthodox or Old-Believer, always religious, dressed in national costume, and uninfluenced by European civilization."[21] Elsewhere he put it as follows:

> On the one hand, there was governmental, imperial, aristocratic Russia, rich in money, armed not only with bayonets but with all the bureaucratic and police techniques taken from Germany. On the other hand, there

21. A. I. Herzen, *Dvizhenie obshchestvennoi mysli v Rossii* (Moscow, 1907), pp. 51–52.

was the Russia of the dark people, poor, agricultural, communal, democratic, disarmed, taken by surprise, conquered, as it were, without battle.[22]

To Herzen and his fellow Russian intellectuals of the mid-nineteenth century, this deep social cleavage appeared a peculiarity of Russian historical experience. In the comparative perspective that another century or so has opened up for us, it no longer seems so. The rift between the "two Russias" may be seen and understood as a particularly sharp manifestation of tendencies that are generally characteristic of societies of arrested and differential modernization. To illustrate by an example far removed from the Russian case in both time and space, present-day Guatemala has been described by a perceptive observer as "two Guatemalas." The center of Guatemala City affords a spectacle of affluence, with foreign cars, amenities of modern life, and dazzling window displays of manufactured consumer goods. But this modern Guatemala belongs to a very small affluent minority that is "culturally alienated" from the peasant majority, most of whom eat only about a third of what they should. The bulk of the country's population, some 40 to 50 per cent of it Indian in origin, lives in the rural highlands under quite primitive conditions. One finds many people "clinging to the ancient tongues, dress, and habits the Spanish found when they came here." The country's planning board estimates that 75 per cent of the country's population "has no access to modern civilization and culture." This means, among other things, that a still higher proportion of rural Guatemalans cannot read or write, and receive little or no

22. Herzen, "Christened Property," in *Izbrannie filosofskie proizvedeniia* (Moscow, 1946), II, 253. For a fuller discussion of the theme of the two Russias in nineteenth-century Russian thought, see "The Image of Dual Russia," in R. Tucker, *The Soviet Political Mind* (New York: Praeger, 1963).

schooling in childhood. The inequality of landholding is indicated by the fact that slightly over 2 per cent of the farms cover more than 70 per cent of the farm area. And the land reform that might change this situation, as well as the taxes that could finance the country's further economic development, are successfully resisted by the small affluent minority that controls both the government and the economy.[23]

Societies of arrested and differential modernization have a revolutionary potential, greater or lesser depending upon historical circumstances unique to each case. The reasons for their proneness to revolution are essentially of two kinds. First, in a country where full-scale modernization is blocked by one or (more likely) a combination of such resistances as those instanced above, revolutionary *political* change, the displacement of the change-resisting dominant social forces from power, becomes the prerequisite of further rapid national development. A gradualistic developmental policy relying upon the existing power structure is extremely unlikely to show success, even with encouragement and assistance from abroad (as under the United States "Alliance for Progress" with Latin America). Given the kind of situation that has been delineated above, the obstructions to the country's integral modernization cannot be overcome without the accession to power of elements deeply committed to this goal. And secondly, such elements do exist in the kind of society under consideration here. A country in which some measure of modernizing change has occurred is virtually certain to possess people of leadership caliber who strongly desire the continuation and completion of the process and are willing or eager to employ revolutionary political means to make this possible.

23. Henry Giniger, "Guatemala Is a Battleground," *The New York Times Magazine,* June 16, 1968, pp. 14, 17, 25. Mr. Giniger was, at the time of writing, Central American correspondent of the *Times.*

The proponents of change come from the educated elite of the society and form a social group that in nineteenth-century Russia acquired the name "intelligentsia." The first generation of the Russian intelligentsia were scions of the landed aristocracy, the so-called "penitent nobles." Representatives of other social classes, particularly including the clergy, joined later. Occupationally the intelligentsia consisted largely of student youth. Education, although a qualification, was not the defining characteristic of the intelligentsia. What set it apart as a special group was, rather, a set of attitudes and values centering in estrangement from their social environment and the desire to change it radically. As Herzen wrote of the young Russians of the 1840's who formed the historical core of the intelligentsia, "The main trait of them all was a deep sense of alienation from official Russia, from the milieu around them, combined with a striving to go out of it, and in some a tempestuous desire to take it along with them."[24] The radical intelligentsia furnished the leadership of the revolutionary movement that developed in Russia during the nineteenth century, and of the revolutionary government that came to power in November, 1917.

An intelligentsia in the sense just discussed is a characteristic feature of society in countries of arrested development. As in nineteenth-century Russia, elements of the educated elite morally secede from their milieu and form themselves into a counter-elite dedicated to radical change. Although they belong by origin to the modernized minority of the society, they identify with the oppressed majority. And despite the fact that it is only a minority of a minority in terms of numbers, the intelligentsia has—as it had in Russia—a potentially very large revolutionary constituency

---

24. Herzen, *Byloe i dumy* (Leningrad, 1946), p. 226. For a full discussion of the intelligentsia in modern Russian history, see especially Richard Pipes, ed., "The Russian Intelligentsia," *Daedalus* (Summer, 1960).

among the masses of the population. Especially under conditions of extraordinary social strain and misery, such as those brought on in Russia by the first World War, a great many of the poor and underprivileged may become responsive to the revolutionary leadership of a determined party of the intelligentsia. At such a time, the revolution-prone society moves into what Lenin called a "revolutionary situation."[25] And if a successful revolution occurs under these circumstances, the group that comes to power will proclaim the further modernization of the country as a supreme goal of its policy.

Strong national feeling is a characteristic element in the makeup of the intelligentsia in an underdeveloped country. That, in large part, is why it resents the country's backwardness, feels enraged by its developmental stagnation, and espouses the cause of its modernization in a passionate revolutionary spirit. That, too, is the source of its typical optimistic faith in the capacity of the nation to contribute to civilization and its desire to build the country up into something that all its citizens might justifiably be proud of. One of the early leaders of the Russian intelligentsia, Vissarion Belinsky, gave classic expression to this attitude when he prophesied in 1840:

> Let us envy our grandchildren and great-grandchildren who are destined to see Russia in 1940—standing at the head of the educated world, laying down laws in science and art, and receiving reverent tribute of respect from the whole of enlightened humanity.[26]

25. For a discussion of this subject, see the following chapter, pp. 130–172.

26. P. I. Lebedev-Poliansky, *V. G. Belinsky. Literaturno-Kriticheskaia deiatel'nost'* (Moscow and Leningrad, 1945), p. 285. In that same year, Belinsky wrote to his friend Botkin: "Things are bad, brother, so bad that life seems not worth living. Cold, apathy, and unconquerable lethargy in the soul. Russian reality oppresses me horribly."

But such pronounced national feeling does not typically bring the intelligentsia of an underdeveloped country to national*ism* as an ideology for the politics of revolutionary change. Nor, on the other hand, is it attracted by an ideology of laissez-faire liberalism, such as accompanied and assisted the rise of a market society in the age of the industrial revolution in the West.[27] In the absence of a rising bourgeoisie with the will and capacity to transform existing conditions and overcome the entrenched interests opposed to full-scale development, a gospel of competitive individualism is useless for modernization. What appears needed to get the underdeveloped country moving is collective effort inspired by a national sense of political purpose. Ideologically, therefore, the intelligentsias of such countries gravitate to one or another of the various doctrines of socialism. And for many, the socialist doctrine with the greatest appeal is Marxism.

The Problem of Appeals

So we come finally to the paradox that the politics of revolutionary change in a society of arrested and differential modernization may be Marxist in ideology. The paradox grows out of the fact that the whole pattern of social history delineated above—comprising the partial development of a traditional society, the slowing down of the developmental process due to resistances to integral modernization, and the revolutionary way out of the situation—is something for which classical Marxism made no provision in its conceptual structure. This is an historical syndrome in

27. On liberalism as an ideology of modernization in West European society in the nineteenth century, see Karl Polanyi, *The Great Transformation* (New York and Toronto: Rinehart & Co., 1944), especially chapters 12 and 13.

which modernization does not ensue from the rise and self-sustained development of capitalist enterprise; in which not the bourgeoisie but an intelligentsia provides the leadership for integral modernization; in which revolutionary political change becomes the *sine qua non* of the process beyond a certain point; and in which, therefore, politics rather than economics is causally primary. Since Marx and Engels contributed relatively little to the scientific understanding of this syndrome, how are we to explain why many would-be modernizers among the intelligentsias of underdeveloped countries have found Marxism congenial as an ideology?[28]

One part of the answer, though probably not the greatest part, is that the Marxian revolutionary idea has a sweep and grandeur missing from other versions of socialism, and appeals to the lively social imagination of an intelligentsia, to its craving for grand historical prospects. As a member of the Russian intelligentsia who was converted to Marxism in the 1890's recalled long after,

> The Marxist movement of the late 'nineties was born of a new vision: it brought with it not only emancipation

28. See Ulam, *The Unfinished Revolution*, for a systematic and stimulating discussion bearing upon this question. I am in broad agreement with Ulam's thesis that Marxism " . . . is the *natural* ideology of underdeveloped societies in today's world," but I do not find convincing his explanation that this results from " . . . the psychology of large masses of the population in a society that undergoes the process of transition from a traditional, preindustrial phase to industrialization. Without having read a word of Marx or Lenin, an illiterate peasant who is being squeezed economically or forced to give up his land and work in a factory experiences almost instinctively the feelings that Marxism formulates in a theoretical language . . . " (pp. 264–265). Without contesting the statement just quoted, I nevertheless believe, for reasons explained above, that the problem of Marxism's impact in underdeveloped countries is chiefly a question of its appeal to members of the intelligentsia, which in turn may become the propagator of Marxism among the masses. If the fulcrum of Marxist influence is an intelligentsia, an explanation based on mass psychology and peasant receptivity in a society undergoing industrialization is critically incomplete. In addition, as noted above, the society in which Marxism acquires influence may not be currently in the throes of industrialization.

from the routine of populism, but also a purpose and a new conception of man. . . . What attracted me most of all was its characteristic appreciation of the moving forces below the surface of history, its consciousness of the historic hour, its broad historical perspectives, and its universalism. The old Russian socialism seemed provincial and narrow-minded in comparison. The fact that Marxism took root among the Russian intelligentsia was evidence of a further Europeanization of Russia and of her readiness to share to the end the destiny of Europe.[29]

As Berdyaev's reminiscences also suggest, another part of the answer to our question is that Marxism provides the radical modernizers with a compelling vision and statement of the social goal. In its conception of future socialism or communism it conjures up a picture of a completely modernized society as the terminus of the historical process. As we have seen in earlier chapters, Marx and Engels envisaged the future scene of man's liberation and self-fulfillment as a society in which the productive powers of modern machine industry would be developed to the fullest extent. To the rustic idylls of such theorists of village socialism as the Russian Populists of the mid-nineteenth century they opposed the projection of an aesthetically-transformed urban setting in which man would have left far behind what the *Manifesto* called "the idiocy of rural life." No matter that the grubby organizational specifics were left out, that there was no detailed prospectus of future arrangements. The inspiring thing was the idea that the liberation and full-scale development of the productive powers, i.e., modernization

---

29. Nicolas Berdyaev, *Dream and Reality: An Essay in Autobiography*, trans. Katharine Lampert (New York: Collier Books, 1950), pp. 119–120. Berdyaev later became known as a non-Marxist religious thinker and interpreter of Russian intellectual history.

in the technological sense, would not only resolve the material problems of society but make possible man's transformation into a new, many-sided, mentally enriched, spiritually matured man of cosmopolitan breadth and horizons. As Trotsky put it in a lyrical passage,

> Man will become immeasurably stronger, wiser and subtler; his body will become more harmonized, his movements more rhythmic, his voice more musical. The forms of life will become dynamically dramatic. The average human type will rise to the heights of an Aristotle, a Goethe, or a Marx. And above this ridge new peaks will rise.[30]

But to explain why Marxism has exerted (and exerts) such influence upon intelligentsia minds in underdeveloped societies, it is essential to go further and show how it may help to orient them in existing circumstances. We must, in other words, see how Marxism's view of the *pre*revolutionary period may plausibly appear burningly relevant to such a society's present predicament and problems. That such could be the case may seem improbable in the extreme. For Marx and Engels pictured the communist revolution developing as a mass movement of rebellious factory workers and proletarianized petty bourgeois in a society of advanced capitalism dominated by the bourgeois class, whereas the society here in question is one that on Marxist criteria would have to be classified as "semifeudal" or at most as "semibourgeois." Thus Russia in the 1890's, when Marxism supplanted the old Populist teaching as the regnant socialist ideology among the intelligentsia, was still fundamentally prebourgeois in its overall socioeconomic character and political structure. Despite the considerable growth of capitalist enterprise and of the factory working class that had

30. Leon Trotsky, *Literature and Revolution* (Ann Arbor: University of Michigan Press, 1960), p. 256.

taken place since the reforms of the sixties, the economy was still predominantly agrarian, peasants accounted for about four-fifths of the total population, the capitalists were far from social supremacy, and the great bureaucratic monarchy in St. Petersburg was an obvious anachronistic monstrosity. So backward was Russian society on the whole that the Marxists generally took it for granted that any revolution in the immediate historical future would necessarily be "bourgeois democratic" rather than proletarian, that its basic mission would be to clear away the debris of Russian absolutism, bring the bourgeoisie to supremacy in society, and set the scene for the full and uninhibited development of capitalism. Yet the *Communist Manifesto*'s picture of society on the eve of *proletarian* revolution had a strangely captivating effect upon their minds; and the same, *mutatis mutandis*, has been the case in other semimodern societies, some of them (for example China) less developed than Russia was at the turn of the century. Why?

The basic reason, I suggest, is that Marxism portrays a totally polarized prerevolutionary society, a society divided into two hostile class camps. The prime characteristic of all past societies, according to the *Manifesto*, has been their division into warring classes, and the distinctive feature of the present epoch is the *simplification* of the class antagonisms: "Society as a whole is more and more splitting up into two great hostile camps, into two great classes directly facing each other: Bourgeoisie and Proletariat."[31] This central theme in Marxism is intensely meaningful to many members of the radical intelligentsia of a semimodern country because of a salient aspect of society as they perceive it around them: its bifurcation. Owing to the impact of differential modernization, the disparity between the mode of life of the minority of well-to-do upper- and middle-class

31. Marx and Engels, *Selected Works*, I, 34–35.

people and that of the great mass of peasants and other lower-class people has become not only visible but glaring. The one group belongs to modern society and enjoys its amenities; the other still lives, to a great extent, as in pre-modern times. And the enormous contrast between the affluence of the one and the poverty and misery of the other is conjoined with such a great cultural gulf that there appear, as we have seen, to be two nations inhabiting one country.

The radical intelligentsia, coming in most cases from the privileged minority, are guiltily and indignantly conscious of the great social cleavage as the most important—and unconscionable—fact of life in their country; and some among them want to take revolutionary action to eliminate it. To them Marx's account of contemporary society speaks volumes. Its description of a social scene dominated by the division between two great classes is relevant to the bifurcated society that they know. Its image of a "more or less veiled civil war raging within existing society up to the point where that war breaks out into open revolution, and where the violent overthrow of the bourgeoisie lays the foundation for the sway of the proletariat,"[32] corresponds to what they would *like* to see happen in their country. And its call to a revolutionary strategy of class struggle is both a theoretical legitimation of their instinctive line of action and a platform with which they can go to the masses as propagandists and agitators.

True, their country's two nations, although divided by class as well as by gross inequalities of wealth and possessions, are not really the two classes of which Marx spoke. The affluent elite is not primarily bourgeois although it includes native capitalists, nor are the poverty-stricken masses primarily proletarian. The former group is largely com-

32. *Ibid.,* p. 45.

posed of landowners; the latter, of peasants. But this circumstance, while it creates problems for Marxism as sociological theory, does not deprive it of great force as political ideology. It does not prevent elements of the radical intelligentsia from seeing their bifurcated society through Marxist eyes, from *assimilating* the realities around them to Marx's vision of class polarization. This is, moreover, all the easier for them when, as in Russia of the 1890's, the further growth of capitalism is slowly lessening the discrepancy between Marxist theory and social reality by increasing the influence of the bourgeoisie on the one hand and the numbers of factory workers on the other.

For illustration we may point to the case of Lenin—a momentous case since he was not only the founder of Russian Bolshevism and the international communist movement of the twentieth century but also the chief formulator of its creed, the communist persuasion in Marxism. A representative of the Russian radical intelligentsia who had acquired from experience and from foregoing generations of Populist revolutionaries the consciousness that there existed two Russias, he found Marxism powerfully attractive in part because of its class-struggle doctrine. And he propounded this doctrine with passionate intensity from his first writings to his last. He spoke in an early pamphlet of "semi-Asiatic Russia," and said that "numerous and varied strata of the Russian people are opposed to the omnipotent, irresponsible, corrupt, savage, ignorant, and parasitic Russian bureaucracy." It was hardly Marx's picture of class war in bourgeois society, yet Lenin proceeded to argue on the same page that the great task for Russian Social Democrats was to unite all their activities "into one whole, into the single *class struggle* of the proletariat."[33] A few years later, in his influential tract *What Is To Be Done?*, he envisaged—again

33. "Tasks of the Russian Social Democrats" (1898), in Lenin, *Selected Works*, I, 139. Lenin's italics.

in Marxist class terms—a struggle between the two Russias in which a party of Marxist revolutionaries would organize and lead a mass movement of disadvantaged Russians from all strata against the Tsarist order, which would be overthrown in a national insurrection. From this position he moved easily, under the impact of the mass upheaval of 1905, to the strategy of seeking, in a democratic revolution against Tsarism, to form a "revolutionary-democratic dictatorship of the proletariat and peasantry." It was the strategy of telescoped revolution that the Bolsheviks, under his leadership and Trotsky's, successfully carried out in 1917.

What is in some ways most striking in Lenin's Marxism is its deep-dyed class orientation. "There are two nations in every contemporary nation," he wrote in a characteristic passage in 1913, and went on:

> There are two national cultures in every national culture. There is the Great-Russian culture of the Purishkeviches, Guchkovs, and Struves, but there is also the Great-Russian culture characterized by the names of Chernyshevsky and Plekhanov. There are *the same two* cultures among the Ukrainians, as there are in Germany, France, Britain, among the Jews, etc.[34]

It was a passage subtly different from anything to be found in the classical Marxist writings. It epitomized the *Weltanschauung* of Lenin as a Marxist from a society wherein the two nations and the two cultures were visibly distinct. He successfully superimposed the class-war doctrine of Marx upon the bifurcated society of semimodern Russia and other societies like it. The later influence of Leninist Marxism in the underdeveloped countries of the world was foreshadowed in this success.

34. *Kriticheskie zametki po natsional'nomu voprosu*, in Lenin, *Sochineniia*, 4th ed. (Moscow, 1950–1956), XX, 16.

Chapter Five

MARXISM AND COMMUNIST REVOLUTIONS

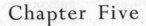

The Postulate of Universality

Classical Marxism projected the communist revolution as a universal phenomenon. The goal it foresaw for *Weltges-chichte* was a planetary communist society wherein man everywhere would realize his essential creative nature, having overcome by the socialization of private property the alienation endured in the course of history. Although the arenas of proletarian communist revolution would be national, the revolutionary movement would not and could not be confined to one or a few major nations but would overflow national boundaries owing to the emergence in the bourgeois period of large-scale machine industry and a world market linking all countries. Thus the *Communist Manifesto* spoke of the communist revolution as occurring initially in "the leading civilized countries at least." In a first draft of the document, Engels had written that "the communist revolution will not be national only but will take place simultaneously in all civilized countries, i.e. at any rate in Britain, America, France, and Germany."[1] The communist revolution would be no less universal than its historical predecessor, the bourgeois revolution, for the world that the proletarians had to win was one that capitalism itself was fast transforming into a socioeconomic unit.

Not surprisingly, the theory of the world communist revolution underwent significant modification in the movement of thought from classical to communist Marxism. In 1915, Lenin laid down "uneven economic and political development" as an absolute law of capitalism and deduced from it that a communist revolution was possible first in several capitalist countries, or even in one. He added:

> The victorious proletariat of that country, having expropriated the capitalists and organized its own socialist production, would stand up against the rest of the world, the capitalist world, attracting to its cause the oppressed classes of other countries, raising revolts in those countries against the capitalists, and in the event of necessity coming out even with armed force against the exploiting classes and their states.[2]

In the wake of the Russian Revolution of February 1917, which overthrew the Tsar, Lenin's party attempted to enact this revoutionary scenario. After they took power in October, however, their efforts to raise revolts in other countries had little success, the revolutionary outbreaks in Hungary and Germany were abortive, and the venture in

1. "Grundsätze des Kommunismus," in K. Marx and F. Engels, *Werke* (Berlin: Dietz Verlag, 1959), V, 374.
2. "The United States of Europe Slogan," in Lenin, *Selected Works*, I, 632.

revolutionary war in Poland in 1920 ended in failure. A Communist International was brought into existence under Russian auspices to promote communist revolutions in other countries, but these showed little sign of materializing.

Despite this fact, the Russian communist mind held tenaciously to the view that the Russian revolution was no mere national event but represented the beginning of a world revolution. "This first victory *is not yet the final* victory," declared Lenin in an address on the fourth anniversary of the October Revolution.

> We have made a start. When, at what date and time, and the proletarians of which nation will complete this process is not a matter of importance. The important thing is that the ice has been broken; the road is open and the path has been blazed.[3]

Even in his very last essay, written in March 1923 in the shadow of approaching death, Lenin optimistically maintained that "the whole world is now passing into a movement which must give rise to a world socialist revolution." Significantly, however, what now sustained his confidence in the final outcome was not the immediate prospect of a communist revolution in "the counterrevolutionary imperialist West" but developments in "the revolutionary and nationalist East." In the last analysis, he wrote, the upshot of the struggle would be determined by the fact that Russia, India, China, etc., accounted for the overwhelming majority of the population of the globe:

> And it is precisely this majority that, during the past few years, has been drawn into the struggle for emancipation with extraordinary rapidity, so that in this respect there cannot be the slightest shadow of doubt what the final outcome of the world struggle will be.

3. "The Fourth Anniversary of the October Revolution," in Lenin, *Selected Works*, II, 751.

In this sense, the complete victory of socialism is fully and absolutely assured.[4]

The universalistic significance of the Russian Revolution remains a basic postulate of communist ideology at the present time. In the opening words of the new Program of the Communist Party of the Soviet Union, adopted in October 1961: "The great October Socialist Revolution ushered in a new era in the history of mankind, the era of the downfall of capitalism and the establishment of communism." The communist revolutions in Asia and Europe following the Second World War are viewed as a continuation of a world revolutionary process initiated in Russia at the close of the First World War, and the process itself is depicted as one that is destined ultimately to embrace the entire world. The Soviet literature on the fiftieth anniversary of the October Revolution stressed this theme heavily and was replete with denunciation of Western scholars for refusing to acknowledge the "world-historical" character of the Russian revolution. Thus, the author of an editorial in the journal of party history dismissed as erroneous the opinion of the American historian Robert V. Daniels that "the Russian revolution was not a national instance of a presumed international trend toward proletarian revolution, but a distinctive national event" and that "with all its international trappings and designs, communism remains a specifically Russian movement, a product of Russian society, Russian ideas, the Russian revolution, and Russian power." The Soviet writer affirmed, in opposition to such a notion, "the indisputable fact that the experience of the first victorious socialist revolution has universal significance, that certain features of the October Revolution reflect basic regularities of social development inherent in our epoch."[5] And the

4. "Better Fewer, but Better," in Lenin, *Selected Works*, II, 854.

5. T. T. Timofeev, "Mezhdunarodnoe znachenie oktiabrskoi revoliutsii i sovremennaia ideologicheskaia bor'ba," *Voprosy istorii KPSS*, 6 (June, 1967), pp. 7, 9.

"Theses" of the C.P.S.U. Central Committee on the fiftieth anniversary stated simply: "The October Revolution marked the beginning of the transition from capitalism to socialism throughout the world."[6]

These contentions raise a series of important theoretical questions that are still in need of clarification and solution. Was the October Revolution the Russian expression of a revolutionary process that is not specifically Russian even though it occurred first in Russia and has been heavily influenced by this fact? Was it the national Russian form of a wider communist revolution going on in the world? If so, is the communist revolution to be seen in universalistic terms, as a developing *world* revolution? What generalizations can be drawn concerning the nature of this world revolution on the basis of the fourteen communist revolutions that have occurred? And finally, is it possible to construct a typology of communist revolutions, with special reference to the manner in which communism comes, or has come, to power? Recognizing that definitive treatment of these questions is beyond the scope of the present chapter, I should like nevertheless to outline some answers and reasons for offering them.

The Revolution of Underdevelopment

Although it originated in Russia and bears a host of Russian birthmarks and influences, communism is not accurately described as a "specifically Russian movement." The familiar analogy with the history of religions remains relevant. A religion that arises in one nation and reflects its spirit can nevertheless spread and take root elsewhere; and it

6. *Pravda*, June 25, 1967.

can do this even though it may initially spread through conquest and forcible conversion. So too with communism as an ideological movement professing "Marxism-Leninism" as its credo. Russia's communist revolution was the first and in some ways the precondition of others that were still to come; and its leaders have striven incessantly to play a hegemonic role in communist revolution wherever it occurs. The spread of communist revolution beyond Soviet borders in the wake of the Second World War was assisted and in numerous countries even engineered by the Soviet Union. Yet the non-Russian communist revolutions cannot be satisfactorily explained as a mere cover for Soviet imperialism or Russian expansion. Communist revolutions enlist indigenous forces in the societies concerned and tend to develop—even when initially imposed from without, as in Rumania—an internal dynamic of their own. There is thus some truth in the Soviet thesis that Russia's communist revolution was only the beginning of a larger process of revolutionary change taking place in the twentieth century, that it was no mere national Russian phenomenon. This does not, however, imply that the communist revolution is destined to become world-wide. In order to pass judgment on that question, it may be of use to inquire into the character of communist revolutions.

It has often been noted—and remains notable—that communist revolutions have not occurred on the model projected by classical Marxism. For Marx and Engels the revolutionary overthrow of bourgeois society was something inherent in the very dynamics of capitalism as a mode of production based on wage labor and the drive to maximize profit. Their complex argument has been examined in an earlier chapter. Suffice it to say that capitalist economic development, in Marx's view, necessarily brings a proletarianization of the masses of factory workers and a progressive worsening of their living and working conditions. Marx formulated it as the "absolute general law of capitalist accumulation" that

> the accumulation of wealth at one pole of society involves a simultaneous accumulation of poverty, labor torment, slavery, ignorance, brutalization, and moral degradation, at the opposite pole—where dwells the class that produces its own product in the form of capital.[7]

At the postulated point in this process at which conditions become wholly intolerable, the masses of workers revolt and the communist revolution occurs with the seizure and socialization of private property. Thus, classical Marxism envisaged the communist revolution as a *revolution of capitalist breakdown* occurring in the most advanced stage of development of the capitalist system. This was the assumption underlying the expectation of Marx and Engels that communist revolutions would come first in the countries of Western Europe where capitalism was most highly developed.

History has diverged in two fundamental ways from their theory. First, capitalist societies, instead of suffering self-destruction in a proletarian upheaval, have gone through a process of self-modification that Marx would not have thought possible and for which his theory in any event made no provision. In violation of the "absolute general law of capitalist accumulation," the industrial worker has won improved conditions and has tended to grow more integrated into the society rather than more alienated from it. Capitalist economies have evolved into postcapitalist mixed economies with self-stabilizing tools of fiscal regulation and planning. Although significant communist movements still exist in some of these societies, Italy and France

---

7. *Capital*, p. 714.

in particular, what prospects they may have of coming to power do not derive from the dynamics of capitalist development. No communist revolution has taken place on the classical Marxist model, and no such revolution seems likely. Indeed, societies that have experienced thoroughgoing capitalist development appear to be among the least likely prospects for communist revolution.

If classical Marxism erred in projecting the communist revolution in a form in which it would not occur, it likewise erred in failing to foresee it in the form in which it *would* occur. The communist revolution has not come about as a revolution of capitalist breakdown; large-scale industrialization has been among its consequences rather than its causes. It does, however, show a certain general pattern. With but two exceptions (Czechoslovakia and East Germany), the typical habitat of communist revolution has been a country of precapitalist or at most semicapitalist economic formation, and one that has shown a tendency to stagnate in its further economic development and modernization. It has been a country heavily populated by peasants and dependent upon agriculture, although usually with at least a small industrial working class and some development of modern industrial economy; a socially and politically as well as economically backward country, with very sharp class divisions and political institutions of traditional authoritarian complexion. Finally, it has been a country with chronic social unrest and a radical intelligentsia ready to furnish the leadership of a mass-based revolutionary movement to overthrow the old order in the name of national renovation and development. Russia and China are both classic cases in all these respects.

The communist revolution—insofar as we can draw a generalization concerning its nature on the basis of these facts—is a *revolution of underdevelopment*, and this in two senses: (1) the revolution typically comes about in the setting of underdevelopment as just described; and (2) it becomes, after the achievement of power by the communist movement, a long-term effort to overcome the country's underdevelopment, a revolution of modernization. The communist revolution is not the sole or necessary form of the revolution of underdevelopment. In some countries, particularly since the end of the Second World War, there have been attempts to carry through such a revolution under noncommunist nationalist leadership, which, however, usually borrows some aspects of communist experience and organizational technique. The most that communism might reasonably claim is to have been so far the most influential and in certain respects the most efficacious form of the revolution of underdevelopment. The notable disadvantage of communism lies in the peculiarly great difficulty that it experiences in coming to power. In the Arab Middle East, for example, the revolution of underdevelopment has proceeded—where it has proceeded at all—under nationalist rather than communist auspices, not because the nationalist political forces can carry it through most successfully but because no indigenous communist movement has been capable of competing with nationalist revolutionary groups in the contest for power.

The Role of War

A further general observation concerning communist revolution relates to international war as its background. If, in a flight of fantasy, we imagine the leading representatives of the capitalist countries coming together in secret conclave around the year 1910 to organize a long-range conspiracy for the prevention of communism, it is easy to see in retrospect what could have proved a simple but quite effective conspiratorial formula: no war. Without the two world wars of our century, it is not at all certain that any communist movement anywhere would have come to power. The fabric of Russian government, economy, and society was so strained by the First World War that Bolshevism, under the inspired leadership of Lenin and Trotsky, was able to maneuver itself to power in the chaotic conditions that ensued with the deposition of the Tsar. It is notable that when news of the February revolution reached Lenin in Switzerland, he immediately saw it as a revolution engendered by the war; and in one of the last of his writings he still spoke of the Russian Revolution as "the revolution that broke out in connection with the first imperialist World War."[8] Moreover, if the initial communist revolution took place in Russia as a result of the First World War, communism came to Eastern and Central Europe, China, Korea, and Vietnam as a direct outgrowth of the Second World War. In some of these cases, Soviet occupation of neighboring lands at the war's end created conditions under which communist regimes could come to power. In other cases, the war so strained the fabric of some societies, most notably China's, that communist revolution could take place in the aftermath independently of Soviet help.

The organic connection between international war and the spread of communist revolution became an axiom of Soviet thought in the Stalin era. Should a new war come, Stalin declared in his report to the Seventeenth Party Congress in 1934, it would be a most dangerous war for the bourgeoisie: "And let not Messieurs the bourgeoisie blame us if some of the governments near and dear to them, which today rule happily 'by the grace of God,' are missing on the morrow of such a war."[9] Still earlier, in a speech delivered to a closed session of the party Central Committee on

8. "Our Revolution: Apropos of the Notes of N. Sukhanov," in Lenin, *Selected Works*, II, 837. For Lenin's reaction when the news of the first revolution reached him in Switzerland, see his "Letters from Afar," in *ibid.*, I, 751.

9. Stalin, *Works* (Moscow, 1955), XIII, 303.

January 19, 1925, Stalin had envisaged the policy that the Soviet Union should follow in event of a new European war. He observed that conditions were maturing for such a war and urged that everything be done to strengthen the Soviet army. Then he went on:

> "Our banner is still the banner of *peace*. But if war breaks out we shall not be able to sit with folded arms. We shall have to take action, but we shall be the last to do so. And we shall do so in order to throw the decisive weight in the scales, the weight that can turn the scales.[10]

In the latter part of the 1930's, Stalin attempted to make events unfold according to this plan by seeking an agreement with Hitler. He knew that the Nazi-Soviet pact of August 1939 would unleash war, but calculated that it would be a long-drawn-out war between the Axis states and the Western allies, a war in which the U.S.S.R. would remain free to "throw the decisive weight in the scales" at a time of its choosing. Stalin's error—an error made by many at the time—lay in overestimating the strength of France, whose swift defeat in 1940 laid Russia open to the invasion that duly followed.[11] But in spite of this terribly costly miscarriage of Stalin's plans, Russia emerged victorious, and communist revolutions took place in numerous countries in the aftermath. The link between international war and the spread of communism was thus still further strengthened in the Stalinist mind, and many Soviet pronouncements in Stalin's last years warned that a third world war would witness the final collapse of the capitalist system. Further-

10. *Ibid.*, VII, 14. This speech was first published when Volume VII of Stalin's works came out in Russian in 1947.

11. For an examination of the evidence in support of this interpretation of Stalin's diplomacy in the 1930's, see the Introduction to *The Great Purge Trial*, ed. R. Tucker and S. Cohen (New York: Grosset and Dunlap Universal Library, 1965).

more, Stalin insisted in his final work, *Economic Problems of Socialism in the U.S.S.R.*, published in 1952, that wars would remain inevitable, as Lenin had written, so long as "imperialism" continued to exist. "To eliminate the inevitability of war," he concluded, "it is necessary to abolish imperialism."[12]

The notion that world communist revolution can continue under peaceful international conditions is a post-Stalinist innovation in Soviet party doctrine. At the Twentieth Party Congress in 1956, the Leninist-Stalinist thesis on the inseparability of imperialism and wars was finally revised; wars were declared to be avoidable calamities in the nuclear age; and the novel idea was put forward that international peace and coexistence might prove propitious for the further spread of communist revolution. "Socialist revolution is not necessarily connected with war," proclaimed the new Soviet Party Program in this connection. "Although both world wars, which were started by the imperialists, culminated in socialist revolutions, revolutions are quite feasible without war." This proposition was accompanied by the thesis—also promulgated at the Twentieth Party Congress—that a communist revolution can, and if possible should, take place by a peaceful parliamentary path. Under favorable conditions, asserted the Party Program, the working class can

> win a solid majority in parliament, transform it from a tool serving the class interests of the bourgeoisie into an instrument serving the working people, launch a broad mass struggle outside parliament, smash the resistance of the reactionary forces, and provide the necessary conditions for a peaceful socialist revolution.[13]

12. Stalin, *Economic Problems of Socialism in the U.S.S.R.* (New York: International Publishers, 1952), p. 30.
13. *Essential Works of Marxism*, ed. Arthur Mendel (New York: Bantam Books, 1961), p. 401.

In various Soviet statements during the Khrushchev era, the Hungarian revolution of 1918–1919 and the communist conquest of power in Czechoslovakia in February, 1948, were cited as historical examples of communist revolution without civil war; and underdeveloped countries with parliamentary institutions were described as the most likely contemporary proving-grounds for communist revolution by the peaceful path. Since the fall of Khrushchev, the doctrine of peaceful communist revolution has been de-emphasized in Soviet writings but not repudiated. It is noteworthy in this connection that the Central Committee's "Theses" for the fiftieth anniversary of the October revolution reaffirmed "the possibility of using, in the transition to socialism, diverse—peaceful and nonpeaceful—forms of struggle, depending on the concrete relationship of class forces in this or that country. . . ."[14]

The new Soviet doctrine on the possibility of peaceful communist revolution has proved highly controversial in the international communist movement and has been one of the central issues in the Sino-Soviet ideological dispute that began in the aftermath of the Twentieth Party Congress. The leader of the Chinese communist revolution, Mao Tse-tung, who had once written that "political power grows out of the barrel of a gun"[15] and continued to believe it, undertook to defend Leninist-Stalinist orthodoxy on the methods of communist revolution against Khrushchevite "revisionism." During the conference of world communist leaders in Moscow in November, 1957, he took a stand on this issue against the effort of the Soviet party leadership to secure adoption of the twentieth-congress line as the general line

14. *Pravda*, June 25, 1967. On the likelihood that the peaceful path would be more feasible in less developed countries than where "capitalism is still strong," see N. Khrushchev, "For New Victories of the World Communist Movement," *Pravda*, January 25, 1961.

15. Mao Tse-tung, "Problems of War and Strategy," in *Selected Works* (New York: International Publishers, 1954), II, 272.

of the world communist movement. In a then secret memorandum to the C.P.S.U. Central Committee outlining views on the question of peaceful transition, the Chinese delegation declared: "We must fully utilize the parliamentary form of struggle, but its role is limited." Using Lenin's line of argument in *The State and Revolution,* the Chinese memorandum stressed that a communist revolution necessitated the destruction of the old state machinery, for which purpose it would not be sufficient to gain a majority in parliament. Hence the communist movement should be prepared to use armed force against the class enemy at the critical juncture of the revolution where power changes hands. In not a single country was the possibility of peaceful transition of any practical significance, and it would not be advisable to place much emphasis upon this possibility in a document published for the guidance of communist parties.[16]

When the controversy came into the open in the early 1960's, the tone was more acrid. The concept of the parliamentary road was now denounced by the Chinese leadership as "parliamentary cretinism." Violent revolution was said to be "a universal law of proletarian revolution." History, argued the Chinese, offered no precedent for peaceful transition to communism. Soviet claims that the October Revolution was "the most bloodless of all revolutions" were totally contrary to historical facts and a mockery of the martyrs who shed their blood to create the world's first communist state. The Hungarian revolution of 1918–1919 was by no means a nonviolent affair or model of peaceful transition, although, as Lenin himself had pointed out, the young Hungarian Communist party had committed the

16. The Chinese memorandum was published in Peking in 1963 after the controversy had come into the open. The text appears in *The Origin and Development of the Differences Between the Leadership of the C.P.S.U. and Ourselves* (Peking, 1963), pp. 58–62.

fatal error of not being sufficiently decisive in the use of force at the critical moment. Nor was the "February event" of 1948 in Prague describable as a "peaceful" conquest of power. And contrary to the "tales of the Arabian nights" being spread by Khrushchev and his ilk, conditions were not now maturing for peaceful transitions to communism. To win a majority in parliament or enter a coalition government owing to electoral success would only be an invitation to the kind of repression that overtook the Chilean Communist party in 1946. Acceptance of the revisionist line against armed struggle had cost the Algerian Communist party a position in its country's political life, and it had led the Iraqi Communist party to disaster in the anticommunist coup in 1958. In sum, "to realize socialism through the 'parliamentary road' is utterly impossible and is mere deceptive talk."[17]

Granted its revolutionary assumptions, the Chinese position is a strong one, just as Lenin's was in his debate with the Social Democrats a half-century ago. If the political essence of a communist revolution is the creation of a one-party state ruled by communists, it is hard to see how it could take place by a peaceful parliamentary path. The previously dominant noncommunist political forces could hardly be expected to submit peacefully not merely to a temporary loss of power but to permanent exclusion from the possibility of regaining it by peaceful means. In order for nonviolent communist revolution to become a real possibility, it would be necessary to devise so insidious a technique of revolution by subversion that the forces being overthrown would hardly be aware of it before it was too late to resist. The fifty-year history of communist revolu-

17. These quotations and paraphrases are taken from *The Proletarian Revolution and Khrushchev's Revisionism* (Peking, 1964), which contains the fullest systematic presentation of the Maoist position on the issue of peaceful transition.

tions contains no instance that would exemplify such a pattern or point to its feasibility.

If peaceful parliamentary transition to communism is unlikely in the extreme, how are we to explain the Soviet espousal of the idea? It can be interpreted as a means by which a no longer radical and, indeed, postrevolutionary Soviet leadership tries to reconcile a continued *verbal* commitment to world communist revolution with a foreign policy whose real first objective is the peace and security of the Soviet Union.[18] Since the further spread of communist revolution would not, in this view, be a serious concern of the Soviet leadership, the unfeasibility of the peaceful parliamentary path would not stand in the way of its espousal in theory. Alternatively, it may be that some Soviet leaders are inclined to see peaceful transition to communism as a more than marginal possibility in historically unprecedented conditions presently taking shape in certain parts of the world, such as the Arab Middle East. They may envisage the revolution of underdevelopment as eventually coming into communist receivership in certain countries where nationalist forces have begun it and where Soviet political influence has been built up through economic and military assistance, diplomacy, and so on. Such a strategic conception may be implicit in a Soviet suggestion that "in present circumstances the question of the possibility of transition to socialism (i.e., to communism) *under conditions of a multiparty system* has topical significance for a number of countries."[19] The local communist party would, in other words, seek participation in a coalition government committed to

18. On this, see chapter 6 below.
19. P. N. Fedoseev, "Velikii rubezh v istorii chelovechestva," *Izvestia,* April 30, 1967, italics added. Fedoseev does not say or imply that the political regime of communist revolution would remain effectively "multiparty" following the transition. A facade of multipartyism could always, of course, be maintained, as it is now in some communist-ruled countries.

carrying through the revolution of underdevelopment; and once it had achieved a foothold in power, it would strive—with judicious Soviet assistance on the side, or with Soviet protection—to maneuver its way to dominance, thereby bringing the revolution from the stage of so-called national democracy to that of "people's democracy," i.e., to communism.

Such, in any event, is one construction that might reasonably be placed upon the Soviet writings in question. Whether the indicated tactics of revolution by political maneuver would have much chance of being applied successfully in practice is another matter. To form a reasoned opinion on this and related questions, it will be useful to examine the various paths that communist revolution has taken in the past.

The Russian Pattern

With respect to the manner of coming to power, the fourteen successful communist revolutions fall into three classes. Russia's communist revolution is in a class by itself. Those in Yugoslavia, Albania, China, Vietnam, and Cuba belong to a second class, that of revolution by armed struggle; and those in Mongolia, North Korea, Poland, Bulgaria, Rumania, Hungary, East Germany, and Czechoslovakia fall into still a third class—the imposed revolution.

The October Revolution was a seizure of power by armed insurrection, carried out in the capital and other main centers at a time of grave national crisis when the government lacked effective control, conditions were chaotic, and masses of people were in a revolutionary mood. The taking of power came at the climax of a period of intensive political preparation during which the Bolsheviks endeavored to stir up revolutionary sentiment with slogans like "land, peace, and bread"; to cultivate mass support in the soviets and the country at large; and to isolate their left-wing competitors, the Socialist Revolutionaries and Mensheviks. The revolutionary *coup* was thus the culminating event in a political process that involved mass agitation and propaganda, maneuvering for position in the soviets, and organization of insurrection.

The relation of town and country, of worker and peasant in the Bolshevik Revolution calls for special attention. In his final written comment on the revolution, Lenin spoke of certain "peculiar features" that distinguished it from earlier revolutions in Western Europe and foreshadowed the pattern the revolution would take in "passing to the Oriental countries." One such feature was the fact that the revolution combined the "peasant war" with the working-class movement under the special emergency conditions created by the World War.[20] The "peasant war" was the upheaval in the countryside during which peasants seized and divided up the remaining landed estates. The encouragement of this action by the Bolsheviks was one of the decisive factors in their revolutionary success, and the agrarian upheaval itself was undoubtedly an essential element of the October Revolution. Yet the countryside was, at least initially, the "rear" of the revolution; the major cities, above all Petrograd and Moscow, were its "front." The revolutionary-minded industrial workers, although only a small minority of the Russian population, nevertheless constituted, along with elements of the armed forces, the spearhead of the Bolshevik movement's mass support, and the main urban centers were the strongholds of revolution. In this sense and to this extent, the October Revolution was "proletarian," as it claimed to be. Without the "peasant war" as its companion-piece,

20. "Our Revolution: Apropos of the Notes of N. Sukhanov," in Lenin, *Selected Works*, II, 838.

it would very probably not have survived in power. But without the working-class support that it received in the chief cities, it could hardly have taken place.

The events of 1917 represented, to a remarkable degree, the fulfillment of a vision of Russian revolution that Lenin had harbored since the turn of the century, when he wrote his seminal work, *What Is To Be Done?* There he contended that socialist revolution would require long preparation and leadership by an elite party consisting chiefly of professional revolutionaries who would inculcate revolutionary ideas in the popular mind by propaganda and agitation. The party was thus conceived as the veritable lever of future revolution. But Lenin did not envisage this revolution as a conspiratorial *coup d'état* to be carried out, as it were, behind the back of the people. The revolution itself, which would ensue after a series of prior revolutionary outbreaks alternating with periods of calm, would be a mass affair culminating in a national armed insurrection against the Tsarist regime. It would draw its motive force from large numbers of nonparty people—workers and others—who would engage in massive insurgency under the guidance and inspiration of the revolutionary party.

St. Petersburg's "Bloody Sunday" in January 1905 touched off a series of revolutionary outbreaks that did not subside until 1907. This revolution of 1905–1907 was perhaps the most spontaneous large-scale insurrectionary movement to be seen in the twentieth century before the Hungarian uprising of 1956, and it influenced Leninist revolutionary thought profoundly. First, it revealed that the peasantry—which Russian Marxists had previously tended to view as a politically inert force and a support for Tsarist despotism—actually possessed a far-reaching revolutionary potential. This in turn brought Lenin to his audacious conception that in a backward country like Russia, which had not yet experienced its "bourgeois revolution," it might be possible to create in the course of such a revolution a "revolutionary democratic dictatorship of the proletariat and peasantry." Here was a crucial component in the developing theory of communist revolution as a revolution of underdevelopment. Further, the 1905 revolution reinforced Lenin's assumption that the final assault upon the old order would come, if ever, at a time of mass revolutionary action and excitement. It confirmed him in the belief that he expressed years later by saying that "revolutions are made at moments of particular upsurge and the exertion of all human capacities, by the class consciousness, will, passion, and imagination of tens of millions, spurred on by a most acute struggle of classes."[21]

In the years between the first and the second Russian revolutions, Lenin elaborated this belief into a theory of the "revolutionary situation." For a Marxist, he wrote in 1915, it is beyond doubt that a revolution is impossible without a revolutionary situation, although such a situation can exist without necessarily giving rise to an actual revolution. There are three principal symptoms of a revolutionary situation. First, a crisis of the policy of the ruling class, creating a crack through which the discontent of the oppressed classes can burst. Next, an aggravation of the sufferings of the oppressed classes beyond the ordinary level. Third, a tendency of these oppressed classes, by virtue of the first two factors, to engage in mass revolutionary action. These views on revolution, added Lenin, "were confirmed particularly graphically for us Russians by the experience of 1905."[22] Never did he abandon them. Indeed, in *Left-Wing Com-*

21. "Left-Wing Communism: An Infantile Disorder," in *Selected Works*, II, 629. In *The State and Revolution*, Lenin wrote that the Russian revolution of 1905–1907 was "undoubtedly a 'real people's' revolution, since the mass of the people, the majority, the 'lowest social ranks,' crushed by oppression and exploitation, rose independently and put on the entire course of the revolution the impress of *their* demands, of *their* attempts to build in their own way a new society in place of the old society that was being destroyed" (*Selected Works*, II, 167).

22. "Krakh II Internatsionala," *Polnoe sobranie sochinenii* (Moscow, 1961), XXVI, pp. 218–219.

munism he formulated it as the "fundamental law of revolution," which had been confirmed by all revolutions,
including three Russian revolutions of the twentieth century, that "only when the '*lower classes*' *do not want* the
old way, and when the 'upper classes' *cannot carry on in the
old way*—only then can revolution triumph. This truth
may be expressed in other words: revolution is impossible
without a nationwide crisis (affecting both the exploited
and the exploiters)." Such a crisis, he went on, is characterized by the fact that at least a majority of the class-con-
scious, politically active workers fully understand that
revolution is necessary and that the ruling classes are going
through a government crisis which draws even the most
backward masses into politics, weakens the government,
and makes it possible for the revolutionaries to overthrow it
rapidly.[23]

It was just such a situation that Lenin saw emerging in the
spring of 1917, in large part because of the Provisional Government's unwillingness to take Russia out of a war that had
become a no longer tolerable burden for masses of the people. "Russia at present is seething," he wrote in early April,
pointing out that "one of the chief symptoms of *every* real
revolution is the unusually rapid, sudden and abrupt increase in the number of 'ordinary citizens' who begin to
participate actively, independently and effectively in political life and in *the organization of the state*."[24] This is what
led him to espouse a maximalist revolutionary policy of no
support for the Provisional Government in the "April Theses" that he put out immediately upon his return from
Switzerland to Petrograd. The dominant trend of opinion
in the Bolshevik leadership in Petrograd was initially resis-
tant, but yielded to Lenin's forceful advocacy of the revo-

23. *Selected Works*, II, 218–219.
24. "The Tasks of the Proletariat in Our Revolution: Draft of a Platform for the Proletarian Party," in *Selected Works*, II, 28.

lutionary slogan "All power to the soviets!" And the further unfolding of events showed the soundness of his perception that Russia was in the midst of a true revolutionary situation which, if properly taken advantage of by the Bolshevik party, could eventuate in a far more radical revolution than the one that had taken place in February.

In presenting the new doctrine of communist revolution by a peaceful parliamentary path, Khrushchev and others have pointed out that for a time in 1917 Lenin believed that the Russian Revolution might take place peacefully in the framework of an assumption of state power by the revolutionary soviets. It is true that in his pamphlet *On Slogans*, written in July, 1917, when the Bolsheviks were under severe harassment by the authorities, Lenin advocated abandonment of the slogan "All power to the soviets" on the ground that it was a slogan for "a peaceful development of the revolution," which had been possible at first but was so no longer.[25] But it is highly questionable whether Lenin ever seriously envisaged a revolutionary consummation without violence. Although revolution to his mind was essentially a process of *political* warfare against a form of society represented and upheld by the existing governmental regime, he appears to have taken it for granted that the final decisive battle—the actual taking of power—would involve armed violence. Not even in a time of crisis, he wrote in the above-mentioned article of 1915, would the old government "fall" without being "dropped."[26] In *The State and Revolution*, on which he worked in August and September of 1917 while in hiding, he corrected Marx's allowance for the possibility of a peaceful revolution in England and America by saying that conditions permitting such a development had changed in those countries since Marx's time; and he formulated it as a general principle that "the replacement of

25. *Selected Works*, II, p. 68.
26. "Krakh II Internatsionala," p. 219.

the bourgeois by the proletarian state is impossible without a violent revolution."[27]

Lenin's preferred title for the violent consummation of revolution at the point where power changes hands was "armed insurrection." In "Marxism and Insurrection," one of his series of secret letters to the party Central Committee in September and October of 1917 urging a *coup* without further delay, he laid the theoretical groundwork. Marxism was distinguished from Blanquism, he argued, not in rejecting the insurrection as a means of revolution, but rather in its insistence that successful insurrection must rely not simply upon conspiracy nor simply upon a party but upon a whole class, and indeed upon the rising revolutionary spirit of the people. Further, insurrection must be launched at the crucial moment in the history of the growing revolution, when revolutionary ferment in the popular ranks is at its height and vacillations in the ranks of the enemies and half-hearted friends of the revolution are strongest. Such a crucial moment was now at hand, he went on. And shortly afterward, in another communication to the same effect, he quoted Marx on the principal rules of insurrection as an art: (1) Never play with insurrection, but see it through to the end; (2) concentrate a great superiority of forces at the decisive point at the decisive moment; (3) once the insurrection has started, act with the greatest determination and take the offensive; (4) try to take the enemy by surprise; and (5) strive for daily successes, even if small. The success of the Russian and world revolutions, Lenin concluded, will depend on two or three days of fighting.[28] So far as the Russian Revolution was concerned, events shortly afterwards proved him right.

27. *Selected Works*, II, 155.
28. "Advice of an Onlooker," in *Selected Works*, II, 133–134. "Marxism and Insurrection" appears in the same volume, pp. 120–124.

The Path of Armed Struggle

"The world-historic significance of the October Revolution," stated the Central Committee's "Theses" on its fiftieth anniversary, "lies in the fact that it pointed out the paths, uncovered the forms and methods of revolutionary transformation, which have acquired an international character."[29] This claim does not find support in the historical record. The October Revolution was the classic communist seizure of power, but it was destined to be a lonely classic, the only successful case of its type in the half-century of communist revolutions that it inaugurated. This, of course, is not to deny that communist revolutions outside Russia have in very many important ways profited from the Russian heritage, Leninist revolutionary theory in particular. Yet the paths taken by the communists of other countries in acquiring power have greatly diverged from that of the first communist revolution. Some of the serious setbacks of communism have occurred as a consequence of unsuccessful efforts to emulate the Russian pattern. And the other thirteen successful communist revolutions have in no instance replicated this pattern.

Among the reasons why the Russian pattern has not repeated itself in other countries, one merits particular attention. The fact is that a "revolutionary situation" in Lenin's sense is an exceedingly rare phenomenon in social history, especially in the highly complex "bourgeois" societies of the present age. Lenin saw revolution as an elemental movement involving millions, occurring at a time of "particular upsurge" when masses of aggrieved humanity were driven by unusually harsh adversity into an insurrectionary mood that

29. *Pravda*, June 25, 1967.

could find outlet in action owing to a partially incapacitating crisis at the top of society and government. Such times of revolutionary crisis have occurred in modern societies, as in Russia in 1905 and 1917, but only as a result of an unusual combination of circumstances inevitably involving an element of fortuity. Lenin himself recognized this when he wrote in *Left-Wing Communism* in 1920 that no amount of propaganda and agitation alone could win over the broad masses to a position of support for the revolutionary "vanguard." "For this the masses must have their own political experience," he went on. "Such is the fundamental law of all great revolutions. . . ." The World War had provided this "political experience" in the immediate past, but what would do it in the coming period? Surveying the postwar scene, Lenin found social life in many countries "crammed full of inflammable material" needing only a spark to be kindled into revolutionary conflagration. Yet he admitted that no one could foretell *"what immediate cause* will most serve to rouse, kindle, and impel into the struggle the very wide masses who are at present dormant."[30] Subsequent history suggests that he may have overestimated the inflammability of the masses in modern society; they have not proved, on the whole, so susceptible to large-scale revolutionary excitement. Ironically, one of the very few true popular upheavals of the ensuing period occurred in communist-ruled Hungary in 1956, where all the elements of a revolutionary situation in Lenin's special threefold sense of the term were present.[31]

Although it did not produce revolutionary situations like the one that came about in Russia in 1917, the Second World War created new opportunities for communist revolution. It might be said to have produced a new *kind* of

30. "Left-Wing Communism," *op. cit.,* pp. 627, 630, 632.
31. This paragraph was written in July, 1967. In the light of subsequent social events in various countries, and most notably the upheaval of May–June, 1968, in France, I am now much less convinced of the relative noninflammability of the masses in contemporary industrial society.

revolutionary situation characterized not by rebellious movements of urban masses but rather by the breakdown of indigenous established authority—particularly in rural areas —under conditions of enemy occupation. The Japanese invasion and occupation of large parts of China in the 1930's, and subsequently of much of Southeast Asia, and the German invasion and occupation of Eastern Europe and the Balkans in the early 1940's provided the setting. Under these conditions, it became possible for communist revolutionary movements to reconstitute themselves as *resistance movements* and to embark upon piecemeal takeovers of the countries by military means, particularly guerrilla warfare. The classic case is, of course, that of China, and Mao Tse-tung, who led Chinese communism to power, is the foremost theorist of communist revolution by armed struggle. With variations growing out of the peculiarities of their national settings, the war-born communist takeovers in Yugoslavia, Albania, and Vietnam also exemplify this pattern, and the Cuban case—although a special one in important respects —is closer to this category of communist revolution than to either of the other two.

A statement of Mao's in 1938 concerning the Chinese prospect forms the best starting point for a comparison of the Russian pattern and revolutions of the Chinese communist type:

> Basically the task of the communist party here is not to go through a long period of legal struggles before launching an insurrection or war, not to seize the big cities first and then occupy the countryside, but to take the other way round.[32]

A difference of relation between town and country, and therefore between worker and peasant, is involved. Instead of a "peasant war" as a companion-piece to the effort to take

32. Mao Tse-tung, "Problems of War and Strategy," in *Selected Works*, II, 267.

power in the chief urban centers, with workers as the revolutionary shock force, we have here a pattern of communist revolution in which the countryside becomes the principal revolutionary arena in the early stages, and in which peasants therefore are the main social base of the revolution. Only in Mao's third strategic stage of revolutionary war, when the guerrilla warfare predominating in the previous two stages of strategic defensive and strategic stalemate gives way to regular warfare in the strategic counteroffensive, do the large cities come into the center of the picture. Their capture is the "final objective of the revolution."[33]

In the earlier stages, the communist-led resistance movement seeks not simply to carry on warfare in the countryside in the manner of historical peasant wars of the roving-insurgents type, but to establish "revolutionary base areas" to function as the rear of the movement. This effort is obviously facilitated in the country concerned by the presence of extensive mountainous, forest, or jungle regions difficult of access by regular troops, and it is notable that all five of the successful communist revolutions of this type have occurred in countries that possess such regions. In the Chinese case, the communist forces established a base area at Yenan after the Long March and then, in the 1937–41 period, created large guerrilla bases in each of the provinces of north China. In Yugoslavia, Tito's partisan forces in the fall of 1941 established a base area in northwest Serbia which became known as the "Uzhice Republic." Later that year they retreated into the relatively primitive mountain areas of Bosnia. In Albania, the communist guerrillas under Enver Hoxha operated in the mountains that cover most of that small land.

In the October Revolution, the taking of power preceded the revolutionary transformation of the sociopolitical order

---

33. Mao Tse-tung, "The Chinese Revolution and the Chinese Communist Party," in *Selected Works*, II, 86. On the three strategic stages, see *Selected Works*, II, 275, 278.

in the country. In the type of communist revolution now under consideration, the revolutionary transformation takes place, or at any rate begins, in the protracted process of conquering power and becomes one of the most important means by which power is then extended. The sociopolitical revolution develops in the liberated base areas, where the communist movement seeks to build not only military strongholds but also enclaves of a new society and policy. Not only are new organs of public authority created, such as the "people's councils" that the Yugoslav communists set up in their base areas and the "democratic governments" that were formed in the north China guerrilla bases, but schools, newspapers, and other social institutions are established under communist auspices. Self-defense corps and "mass organizations" for peasants, youth, women, children, and other groups are founded as means of enlisting people into participation in public life under communist guidance. All this serves the needs of "political mobilization," which Mao described as the promotion of anti-Japanese resistance by telling the people about the political objectives of the war, viz., the ousting of the Japanese and the building of a new China.[34] Thus, military operations go hand in hand with a piecemeal process of nation-building. Guerrilla warfare creates a territory for political mobilization of the populace, which in turn augments the communist resistance forces and makes it possible to expand military operations into new areas. The results are most impressive in the Yugoslav and Chinese cases. By February 1945, Tito's partisan army consisted of fifty-four divisions numbering 800,000 troops. By the time of Japan's capitulation in 1945, one-fifth of the population of China was living in the communist-controlled revolutionary base areas. The official proclamation of the communist government in China on October 1, 1949, marked not the beginning of the communist revo-

34. Mao Tse-tung, "On the Protracted War," in *Selected Works*, II, 204–205.

lution there but the climax of one that had been in progress for upward of a decade.[35] The communist-Kuomintang civil war of 1947–49 was no more than a last act in the drama, the completion of a revolutionary takeover that had already been largely accomplished in the period of anti-Japanese resistance and its aftermath.

As is best shown in the Chinese case, communist resistance movements face a difficult problem with regard to agrarian policy in the revolutionary base areas. In December 1939, Mao declared that since the peasantry was the main force in the Chinese revolution, it must be given help in overthrowing the feudal landlord class. Distribution of the landlords' land among the peasants was one of the programmatic measures of the revolution in its ongoing "new-democratic" or presocialist phase. On the other hand, he likewise stipulated that private capitalist enterprises should be preserved and that "rich-peasant economy should not be eliminated."[36] The policy actually followed by the party during the period of the anti-Japanese war was a moderate one of reducing rents and interest owed by the peasants to the landlord. Radical measures of land redistribution were avoided for fear of alienating large elements of the very peasant population that the resistance movement looked to as its prime source of recruits and general support. As Chalmers Johnson has said, the economic policies of the communists during the Sino-Japanese war were designed to create maximum unity for national defense.[37]

35. Chalmers Johnson, *Peasant Nationalism and Communist Power* (Stanford: Stanford University Press, 1962), p. 1.
36. Mao Tse-tung, "The Chinese Revolution" *op. cit.*, pp. 87, 96–97. See also his subsequent statement in "On New Democracy," in *Selected Works*, III, 122: "In the rural areas, rich-peasant economic activities will be tolerated." These statements presupposed a fourfold classification of the rural population into the landlord class, the rich peasants or rural bourgeoisie, the middle peasants, and the poor peasants *ibid.*, pp. 88, 92–93).
37. Johnson, p. 19.

Chinese communism, like the other communist movements that have come to power by the road of wartime
resistance, built its mass following among the peasants (and
other strata) primarily on the basis of an appeal to nationalism, the patriotic desire to liberate the country from the
foreign invader. The political mobilization of the Chinese
peasants after 1937 proceeded chiefly in terms of the anti-
Japanese slogan of "national salvation." Similarly, the partisans appealed to the Yugoslav peasants with patriotic antifascist slogans mainly aimed against the Germans. In both
instances, the communists took a more militant stance in the
resistance than their rivals (the Kuomintang and Mihail-
ovic's Chetniks), engaging in bold operations that provoked
from the foreign occupiers harsh reprisals that in turn
helped destroy the remaining fabric of the old society and
made the peasants all the more amenable to patriotic mobilization. In wartime Albania, the communist guerrillas used
patriotic antifascist slogans similar to those of the Yugoslav
partisans. After the defeat of Japan, the Vietnam communists espoused Vietnamese nationalism against the French—
and more recently have done so against the U.S. The Castro
movement is exceptional among the guerrilla movements
that have won power both in that its communist alignment
came afterward and in that there was no foreign occupation
against which to mobilize the population. There was, however, a history of American domination of the country, as
well as an oppressive Cuban regime that could be identified
with American influence. The political mobilization of the
Cuban lower classes in the post-revolutionary period has re-
lied heavily upon the slogan of Cuban national independence
against "Yankee imperialism."

So far-reaching is communism's identification with nationalism in this pattern of revolution that an actual fusion
has been hypothesized. Noting that both Chinese and Yugoslav communism were legitimized by the nationalistic cre-

dentials established by the communist parties during the resistance, Chalmers Johnson suggests that the resulting Chinese and Yugoslav governments are the "offspring of indigenous nationalism" and that in both cases the communist ideology "serves as the theoretical expression of these nationalisms."[38] Such an interpretation appears unnecessarily extreme and overlooks the alternative possibility that we have to do here with movements of authentic communist ideological affiliation which have identified themselves with national goals in the process of winning power and at the same time have retained a strong nationalist orientation. In this connection, it must be pointed out that in the Russian revolution we see a very different relationship of the communist movement to nationalism. Here communism came to power on an antiwar platform. Far from identifying itself with Russian national aims in time of war, the Bolshevik movement used the slogan of revolutionary internationalism. From the outbreak of war in 1914, Lenin advocated revolutionary defeatism, the transformation of the international "imperialist war" into a series of revolutionary civil wars inside the warring countries, his own included. "Defensism" became a Bolshevik term of opprobrium for Russian socialists who supported the national war effort. Only in the postrevolutionary period, and particularly under Stalin, did Russian communism take on a pronounced Russian nationalist orientation.

A final comparative observation has to do with the role of armed force in communist revolution. Where the main form of struggle is war and the main form of organization is the army, as in China, the notion of revolution by armed

---

38. *Ibid.*, p. 184. Elsewhere Johnson speaks of "the nationalistic basis of communism in the independent communist states" (*ibid.*, p. 179) and states that "communism and nationalism were fused in wartime China and Yugoslavia as a result of the identification of the CCP and YCP, respectively, with the resistance movements of the two countries . . ." (*ibid.*, p. 8).

struggle can easily become an obsession. Whoever wants to seize the political power of the state and to maintain it must have a strong army, declared Mao in 1938, and he went on: "Some people have ridiculed us as advocates of the 'omnipotence of war'; yes, we are, we are the advocates of the omnipotence of the revolutionary war, which is not bad at all, but is good and is Marxist." Observing further that everything in Yenan had been built up by means of the gun, he added:

> Anything can grow out of the barrel of the gun. . . . With the help of guns the Russian communists brought about socialism. We are to bring about a democratic republic. Experience in the class struggle of the era of imperialism teaches us that the working class and the toiling masses cannot defeat the armed bourgeois and landlords except by the power of the gun; in this sense we can even say that the whole world can be remolded only with the gun.[39]

It is difficult to picture Lenin recognizing this as an authentic voice of Marxism or agreeing with the implied view of the Russian communist revolution. As noted earlier, armed insurrection was a vital ingredient in the Leninist theory and practice of communist revolution. For Lenin, however, the revolutionary process was fundamentally political rather than military in nature. It was the politics of taking power in a society brought by an unusual combination of stresses to a state of turmoil and incipient breakdown. In harmony with his essentially political vision of the revolution, Lenin saw the armed insurrection itself as "a *special* form of the political struggle."[40] It was the *coup de grace* that the revolutionary movement would have to administer

---

39. Mao Tse-tung, "Problems of War and Strategy," in *Selected Works*, II, 272, 273.
40. "Advice of an Onlooker," in *Selected Works*, II, 133.

to the regime it sought to replace, an episode of planned violence at the conclusion of the political struggle. But what about the place of the civil war in the Russian Revolution? It is true that shortly after the Bolshevik seizure of power, Russia became the scene of a three-year bloody civil war in the course of which the revolution took to arms, created its Red Army under Trotsky, and defeated the forces that took the field against it. If the Russian Revolution is viewed as a social epoch, the civil war of 1918–1921 must be considered an integral part of it. However, the civil war, important as it was historically, was not an element in Lenin's *strategy* of revolution. It was forced upon the Bolshevik regime by the efforts of various forces in Russia, aided from abroad, to overthrow it. From a Leninist point of view, especially as shaped by the Russian experience, the need to wage a protracted armed struggle to preserve the power won by revolution is a contingency with which every communist movement must reckon. But such an armed struggle is not seen as either inevitable or desirable, and the gun barrel is not seen as the sole significant source of revolutionary power. To this limited extent, the post-Stalin Soviet theory of a peaceful path can authentically claim a Leninist ancestry.

The Imposed Revolution

In both patterns of communist revolution examined above, the revolution is basically an internal process in the country concerned. This is not to deny that the Soviet Union rendered significant assistance (along with some disservices) to the communist revolutions in countries like China and Yugoslavia. But the assistance was not decisive; at most it was supplementary, and the revolutions in question could have taken place without it. Like the Russian Revolution in its time, these revolutions fundamentally made their way on their own. In contrast, the communist regimes in Mongolia, North Korea, Bulgaria, Rumania, Hungary, Poland, East Germany, and Czechoslovakia did not come to power in basically indigenous revolutions. These communist revolutions were imposed from outside. In all instances save the first, they were engineered by the Soviet Union under conditions of military occupation or domination arising out of the Soviet victory in the Second World War. One could, of course, add to the eight instances of communist revolution just noted the cases of the three Baltic countries, on which communist revolution was imposed in 1940 during the period of the Stalin-Hitler pact. It is, perhaps, all the more important to mention these three instances, since the experience in the Baltic countries, as well as in the areas detached from Poland in 1939, was a forerunner of the process of imposed revolution as it developed after World War II throughout much of Eastern and Central Europe. For Stalin, the Baltic countries were proving-grounds of imposed communist revolution.

Although Marxism-Leninism has contemplated the revolutionary war across national boundaries as one possible form of just war (and the Soviet march into Poland in 1920 stands as an historical example of this form of action), the doctrine assumes that the country invaded would be in the throes of an internally generated revolution or "revolutionary situation" at the time. The forcible imposition of communist revolution upon a country from outside not only lacks sanction in Soviet ideology but has many times been explicitly disavowed as an aim. In Stalin's famous statement to Roy Howard in 1936, "The export of revolution is nonsense."[41] Yet, without ever admitting it, the Soviet

41. Quoted in *Pravda*, Mar. 5, 1936.

Union has practiced such "nonsense" on a large scale. Insofar as conditions in that primitive nomadic country permitted, communist revolution was engineered in Outer Mongolia following the military conquest of the area by the Soviet Union in the early 1920's. In 1939–1940, not long after Stalin's remark to Roy Howard, the communist system was forcibly installed in Soviet-occupied eastern Poland and the three Baltic states. And in the aftermath of the Second World War, Soviet satellite regimes of "people's democracy" were established in North Korea and in Eastern and Central Europe, wherever Soviet power predominated.

The devastation and dislocation of war did much to destroy or greatly weaken the prewar sociopolitical order in Eastern Europe. Although revolutionary situations in the Leninist sense did not exist at the war's end, it was widely accepted among the peoples and political parties that restoration of the *status quo ante* was out of the question and that social change was in order. Yet the communist movements in these countries had little chance of coming to power independently on the tide of change. It is true that communism had not been a negligible indigenous force in prewar Eastern Europe. Communist movements of varying strength had existed in spite of domestic repressions and the loss of many of their leaders in Stalin's purges of 1936–1938, and they carried on underground activities during the war. The Polish Communist party, which had been formally dissolved in 1938 at the height of the Soviet purges, was reconstituted in 1942 and played a part, although a relatively minor one, in the Polish resistance movement. In Czechoslovakia, where communism had shown real strength in the democratic pre-Munich period, underground communists were active in the Free Slovakia resistance movement in 1944. But nowhere in Eastern Europe (outside of Yugoslavia and Albania) did local communists achieve a politically commanding position under war conditions. Only in Czechoslovakia, through a combination of favorable circumstances, did they emerge at the war's end in great strength. There the communists gained control of key posts, including the ministries of interior (police), agriculture, and information; and the communist leader Gottwald became premier after his party polled 38 per cent of the vote in the parliamentary elections of May 1946, the first held after the war. Significantly, however, Czechoslovakia, from which the Soviet army was withdrawn in December 1945, was at the beginning of 1948 the only country in the region not yet under total or near-total communist domination.

In Poland, Bulgaria, Rumania, Hungary, and East Germany, where Moscow was in a controlling position because of the continued presence of its military forces, communist rule was imposed in a process that showed local variations but was everywhere the same in basic pattern. The communists sought to enlarge their popular support by taking charge of land reform or, as in Poland, by exploiting the large patronage opportunities inherent in the postwar resettlement of Poles in the western lands detached from Germany. Meanwhile, under Soviet direction and with Soviet assistance, they acquired strategic positions in the coalition governments initially formed, and drove for ascendancy. Uncooperative political forces, such as the peasant parties that enjoyed strong support in a number of those countries, were pressured, harassed, or simply terrorized in the process. Noncommunist leaders like Maniu in Rumania, Petkov in Bulgaria, and Mikolajczyk in Poland were imprisoned, executed, or hounded out of their countries. Social Democratic parties were deprived of their autonomy and eliminated as possible rivals through forced mergers with the communists in communist-controlled united worker parties. Public organizations were purged of leaders not amenable to communist direction. Gradually the coalition governments were transformed into pseudo-coalitions dominated by the communists, and then into opposition-free regimes on the Soviet model.[42] These communist revolutions from above were completed in all essentials by 1947–1948.

Although not occupied by Soviet forces, Czechoslovakia was ringed by lands that were, and thus it had no access to effective assistance from the noncommunist world. The Soviet military presence on the Czech frontiers, significantly activated at the time, formed the backdrop for the communist action of February 1948 in Prague. With the backing of Premier Gottwald, the communist Minister of Interior ignored an instruction from the majority of the cabinet that he stop packing the police with communists, whereupon ministers belonging to two of the government parties resigned in protest. In the ensuing cabinet crisis, the communists, acting by both constitutional and extraconstitutional means, sent armed detachments of workers into the streets and put pressure on President Eduard Benes, then an old and sick man, to form a new government of predominantly communist complexion. After Benes yielded on February 25, the communist takeover of all power in Czechoslovakia proceeded swiftly. As noted earlier, post-Stalin Soviet writings have cited this as an example of communist revolution by the peaceful parliamentary path. It is true that no civil war occurred. But the *coup de Prague*, which bears a certain resemblance to the pattern of "legal revolution" by which Hitler's National Socialist party took power in Germany in 1933, involved the ruthless application of political coercion and a scarcely veiled threat of armed violence. To call the Czech revolution "peaceful" would unduly stretch the meaning of that word, and references to its path as "parliamentary" should not obscure the

42. For a detailed, country-by-country description of the process, see Hugh Seton-Watson, *The East European Revolution* (New York: Praeger, 1951), especially ch. 8.

fact that it led immediately to the suppression of parliamentary democracy in Czechoslovakia.

One other feature of the imposed communist revolution as it developed in Eastern Europe after the Second World War was the satellization of the communist regimes that arose. Stalin, then at the apogee of his dictatorship, demanded not only communist regimes but dependably subservient ones. Communist governments of relatively independent persuasion, pursuing their national paths of communist development, were no more acceptable to him, perhaps even less so, than noncommunist governments. Accordingly, the Soviet authorities made every effort from the very outset to guarantee Soviet control over the emerging communist regimes. Thus, Soviet advisers were installed in key positions in the police, the army, and other ministries of the governments, and the countries concerned were placed in relations of economic dependency upon the Soviet Union. To ensure cooperation of the local communist authorities in these and similar measures, political responsibility was entrusted as much as possible to thoroughly reliable communist cadres, typified by Matthias Rakosi and Walter Ulbricht, who had spent the war years in Moscow. Initially, however, these "Muscovites" shared positions of power with communist leaders who had worked in underground resistance movements in their own countries during the war, men like Gomulka in Poland, Kostov in Bulgaria, Rajk in Hungary, and Patrascanu in Rumania. Tendencies toward what later came to be called "national communism" were strong in the latter group. Although not at all anti-Soviet and no less serious and rigid in their communist ideological convictions than others in the movement, some communist leaders who had stayed in their countries were inclined—like Tito—to resent Soviet tutelage and dictation of their policies, to place a high priority upon the interests of communism in their own national context, and to adapt the Soviet communist pattern in various particulars to local conditions.

In the new phase of the East European revolution signalized by the creation of the Cominform and by Moscow's anti-Tito declaration of June 1948, Soviet control over the newly established communist regimes was tightened. Stalin's move against Tito was probably intended not merely to provoke the overthrow of the Titoist leadership group in Yugoslavia but also to inaugurate a systematic campaign against national-communist tendencies in Eastern Europe. In the wake of the unexpected failure to force the change in Yugoslavia, the campaign developed into a general purge of "national communists" in other countries of the area. In Soviet-engineered purge trials, Kostov, Rajk, and others were condemned for alleged "nationalist deviationism." In a typical accusation, the Bulgarian communist leader George Dimitrov (a "Muscovite") attributed to Traicho Kostov the "shameful assumption" that Soviet interests might ever be opposed to Bulgarian interests. The purges of communists in 1948–1952 consolidated the position of the "Muscovites" in the East European regimes and generally underscored Soviet dominance in the area. Even the fact that communist revolution had been made possible by the presence of the Soviet army was openly acknowledged and emphasized. Thus, the preamble of the new Polish constitution adopted in 1952 stated: "The historic victory of the U.S.S.R. over fascism liberated Polish soil, *enabled the Polish working people to gain power*, and made possible the rebirth of Poland within new just frontiers."[43]

Satellization of the regimes created by the communist revolution in its Soviet-imposed version would not appear to have been something necessarily inherent in this pattern

43. *Ibid.*, p. 373. Italics added.

of revolution. But owing to a number of factors, chief among which was the personality of the man directing the process, Stalin, revolution could not be exported after the Second World War without the newly established political enterprises' being treated as Soviet property. Not only were communist regimes forcibly imposed upon countries where communism was not strong enough to come to power on its own; a whole system of measures was carried out to prevent these regimes from, so to speak, "nationalizing" themselves by developing policies that would reflect the special needs and circumstances of their countries. This went against the current of tendencies inevitably present within those regimes themselves irrespective of the political fortunes of this or that leader of national-communist leaning. It added to the stigma of foreign origin the onus of continued foreign dependency. Consequently, the post-Stalin relaxation of Soviet dictatorship at home and abroad has been accompanied by an independence movement of varying strength in countries where communism was imposed at the war's end. Even without the Yugoslav example to inspire it, this movement would undoubtedly have emerged when conditions made it possible. The results have so far been mixed. In spite of that, they suggest the hypothesis that communism in power, regardless of how it acquires power, has a tendency to turn into national communism.

The Future of Communist Revolution

A priori schemes of world history aside, the future of communist revolution is no more scientifically predictable in the present state of knowledge than is the future of any other major political phenomenon of our time. However, the comparative study of communism and communist revolutions does suggest some tentative general conclusions that bear upon future prospects:

1. The fact that communist revolution has spread to about a third of the world in its first fifty years does not imply that it will spread, in time, to the remaining two-thirds. There is no good reason to believe that something that could be called a "world communist revolution" is in progress.

2. Neither, on the other hand, would it be justified to assume that no more communist revolutions will take place anywhere. Communist movements of varying strength and vigor exist in over eighty noncommunist countries. Depending upon internal and external circumstances, some may be or may become sufficiently strong to represent potential regimes of communist revolution. Yet in no instance, with the possible exception of South Vietnam, does this now appear an inevitable or overwhelmingly probable eventuality.

3. The communist revolution is likely to preserve its character as a revolution of underdevelopment. Any future communist revolutions will probably occur not in developed industrial countries with advanced social and political institutions, but, as in the past, in underdeveloped countries where economic progress is slow or stagnant, where society is divided into a privileged minority and a disadvantaged peasant majority, and where authoritarian government prevails. There is no law that the revolution of underdevelopment must take place under communist auspices. Noncommunist leadership of it is possible, particularly with encouragement from influential noncommunist powers. However, the prospects for such leadership (and such encouragement) remain highly uncertain.

4. So far as communism's path to power is concerned, none of the three historical variants considered above can be automatically ruled out as a future possibility. But for

various reasons, neither the path of Russia's October Revolution nor the pattern of imposed revolution appears very likely to furnish a model in the future. In underdeveloped countries, the communist road to power through armed struggle and identification with nationalism may prove the highroad. Nor should communism's discovery of new roads to power be excluded, although reasons have been cited here for not expecting the "peaceful parliamentary path" to be one of them. A possible future path, which may have been foreshadowed in the Castro revolution in Cuba, is that of "communism by conversion," where a movement of predominantly nationalist and leftist complexion takes power and subsequently opts for Marxism-Leninism and communist political affiliations.

5. Owing in part to the tendency of communist movements and regimes to acquire a nationalist coloration, communism in power, contrary to the founding ideological prophecies, has not proved a cohesive force internationally. The spread of communist revolution beyond Russia has led to growing polycentrism and to diverse intercommunist divisions and discords, of which the Sino-Soviet conflict has been the most serious. The disintegration of international communism is in some sense a symptom of crisis. But it should not be assumed that this development is in all respects detrimental to communist movements not yet in power. It may, on the contrary, be of assistance to some of them, by compelling them to rely more upon their own efforts and to chart their own paths, and by helping them to escape the onus of foreign inspiration and dependency. The future prospects of communist revolution are not necessarily negated by division in the communist world.

Chapter Six

THE

DERADICALIZATION

OF MARXIST

MOVEMENTS

◇◆◇◆◇◆◇◆◇◆◇◆◇◆◇◆◇◆◇◆◇◆◇◆◇◆◇◆◇

Marxism-Leninism, as the Soviet Marxist ideology is called, has never been wholly static; it has evolved over the years by a process of accretion, elimination and redefinition of dogma. But in the first post-Stalin decade, there were changes of unusual scope and significance in this sphere, accompanying and in some ways mirroring the general processes of systematic change which Stalin's death precipitated in Soviet society. This chapter seeks to interpret the post-Stalin Soviet ideological changes, especially as they bear upon the politics of world revolution. In doing so, it attacks the broader theoretical problem of what goes on in radical political movements and their ideologies as these movements settle down and accommodate themselves to the existing world. For some such tendency appears to be involved in the Soviet case.

Interpretations of Post-Stalin Ideological Change

The year 1956 was the watershed of post-Stalin ideological change in the U.S.S.R. In the Central Committee's report to the Twentieth Party Congress—the first congress held after Stalin's death—Nikita Khrushchev announced a series of doctrinal innovations affecting particularly the line of communist Marxism on international relations and the further development of the world communist revolution. One was the revision of the Leninist thesis on the inevitability of periodic wars under imperialism. On the ground that the world-wide forces for peace were now unprecedentedly strong, it was proclaimed that wars, while still possible, were no longer fatally inevitable even though "imperialism" continued to exist in large areas. Not only could the antagonistic socioeconomic systems peacefully coexist; they could and should actively cooperate in the maintenance of peaceful relations. At the same time, coexistence was a competitive process, economics being the principal arena of competition. In the long-range nonmilitary contest for influence, the communist countries would strive to show the superiority of their socialist mode of production over the capitalist mode and would thereby make the communist socioeconomic model compellingly attractive, particularly to the developing countries. Communism would spread, then, not by force but by force of example. And even as a strictly internal process in the countries concerned, the communist revolution no longer need necessarily be accomplished through large-scale armed violence. New nonviolent forms of "transition to socialism" (i.e., to communism) might be found, especially in countries where capitalism was not yet very strong. Notwithstanding the Leninist tenet that ruling classes do not voluntarily surrender their power, it might now be possible for socialism to come to power in various places by a parliamentary path. The revolutionary forces would strive to "win a firm majority in parliament and to turn the parliament from an agency of bourgeois democracy into an instrument of genuinely popular will."[1]

Such was a large part of what came to be known in the communist world as the "Twentieth Congress line." There were other elements as well. One was the proposal for *rapprochement* and cooperation between communist parties and their historic Marxist enemies, the Social Democratic parties. Another was the formal recognition of Yugoslavia as a member of the family of communist states, and therewith the recognition of diversity in communist methods and institutions as legitimate within certain limits. The Twentieth Congress line was, moreover, accentuated and further elaborated in a series of important Soviet pronouncements in the ensuing years. In elaborating the new thesis on the noninevitability of wars in the present era, Soviet leaders argued that the rulers of the noncommunist powers, or the more moderate and sober elements among them, could perceive the unprecedented dangers implicit in the rise of nuclear weapons and were inclined to take account of these dangers by pursuing a foreign policy designed to avoid another major war. Accentuating the optimistic idea that competitive coexistence could remain peaceful, the Twenty-First Soviet Party Congress in 1959 declared in its resolu-

1. *Pravda,* Feb. 15, 1956.

tion that "even before the complete triumph of socialism on earth, while capitalism still exists on a part of the globe, a genuine possibility will arise of excluding world war from the life of human society."[2] To be sure, "national-liberation wars" were proclaimed to be legitimate and deserving of assistance from communist states. But at the same time, Soviet leaders warned against the dangers of escalation inherent even in small local armed conflicts, and advocated that independence be granted to peoples still under alien rule so that armed struggle would not be needed to attain this goal. And the idea of the desirability of peace-keeping cooperation between competitors, particularly the Soviet Union and United States as the military superpowers of the two coalitions, was elaborated at length in Soviet writings.[3]

Non-Nuclear

The Twentieth Congress line also gave strong endorsement to a new Soviet policy of *rapprochement* with noncommunist nationalist revolutionary regimes and movements in newly independent nations of Asia, Africa, and Latin America. Governments of countries outside the communist bloc were invited to join an expanding world-wide "peace zone" by adopting the policy of nonalignment with existing military blocs. Neutralism, the very possibility of which had been denied in Moscow in Stalin's final years, was thus given Soviet support; and what has come to be called the "third world" was recognized as such in a new tripartite world-view which contrasted sharply with the Stalinist bifurcation of the contemporary political universe into two warring camps. That the developing countries would eventually develop into communist states was postulated, but it came to be recognized that nations choosing the "noncapitalist path" of development might inaugurate socialist

2. *Current Soviet Policies III*, ed. Leo Gruliow (New York: Columbia University Press, 1960), p. 214.

3. For details, see "Dialectics of Coexistence," in *The Soviet Political Mind*.

economic practices in various different ways and not necessarily under communist party auspices. Moreover, a political waystation on the long journey to communism was envisaged in the concept of a "national democracy," which was defined as a noncommunist regime committed to internal developmental goals, tolerant of its own communist movement, and friendly to the Soviet Union and associated states. Soviet writings meanwhile continued to emphasize the possibility of a peaceful parliamentary path of transition to communism. And the association of communism with the idea of dictatorship and violence was further softened with the introduction in 1961 of the notion that the contemporary Soviet state had ceased to be a "dictatorship of the proletariat" and become a "state of the whole people" in continual process of democratization.

All these doctrinal modifications were formally incorporated into the new C.P.S.U. Program adopted by the Twenty-Second Party Congress in 1961. Taken in their interrelated entirety, they marked the passage of Soviet Marxist ideology into a new stage of its history. In the decade since the Nineteenth Party Congress of 1952, which met in Stalin's presence and under his aegis, orthodox Leninism-Stalinism had been supplanted with a new Soviet ideological amalgam which might be called "neocommunist Marxism." Needless to say, it showed continuity with the past, as in the reaffirmation of the ultimate goal of a world communist society. On the other hand, there were definite breaks with the communist ideological past. The doctrines of the non-inevitability of wars and the parliamentary path to communism were deviations from Leninist-Stalinist orthodoxy as derived from such fundamental works of Lenin as *Imperialism* and *The State and Revolution*. The idea of a non-class all-people's state deviated not only from Leninism-Stalinism but from its classical Marxist premises, one of which held that the state qua state is a class agency of repression. And old ideological concepts had in some cases been infused with new content. The most notable example is the altered conception of coexistence, which had once been pictured as a condition of unremitting political warfare and was now seen as a long-range peaceful competition of socio-economic systems for predominant world influence. True, the peacefully coexisting systems were envisaged as remaining adversaries between which no "ideological coexistence" would be possible.

The rise of neocommunist Marxism in the Soviet Union has stimulated a world-wide debate over the meaning of the ideological changes. Three broad lines of interpretation have emerged. One is the official Soviet position, which holds that the ideological changes of the post-Stalin period are simply a new stage in a regular process of adaptation and development of Marxism-Leninism to keep it in tune with changing historical realities. Soviet ideology, according to this view, is a "creative Marxism-Leninism" that does not and cannot go unchanged in various particulars although it always remains true to its foundation principles. In particular, such profoundly important developments of the middle twentieth century as the spread of the communist system and the rise of nuclear weapons necessarily affect the validity of such an ideological thesis as that concerning the inevitability of wars under imperialism. In Khrushchev's words, "one cannot mechanically repeat now what Vladimir Ilyich Lenin said many decades ago regarding imperialism, or continue asserting that imperialist wars are inevitable until socialism triumphs throughout the world." And he went on: "We live in a time when we have neither Marx nor Engels nor Lenin with us. If we act like children who study the alphabet by compiling words from letters, we shall not go very far."[4]

4. *Speech to the Third Congress of the Rumanian Workers' Party, June 22, 1960* (New York: Crosscurrents Press, 1960), pp. 27, 28.

The dominant Western interpretation of the post-Stalin ideological changes is not wholly dissimilar to the Soviet view. Impressed by the vigor of Soviet reaffirmations of commitment to the ultimate goals of world communism, many Western students of Soviet affairs have tended to interpret the ideological innovations as essentially tactical. What has changed to some extent, according to this conception, is the Soviet doctrine on the ways and means of achieving the world communist society that remains the cherished end of Soviet communists. Moreover, the tactical changes represent to a very large extent a forced adjustment of doctrine (and practice) to the necessities of the nuclear age. Because of the enormity of the dangers posed by general war in the present era, the Soviet leadership has been compelled to reconsider its working assumptions concerning the feasible methods of spreading communism. The modified communist credo, with its emphasis upon peaceful competition of systems and its discovery of a peaceful path to communist revolution, has resulted.

A third interpretation, which has been advanced by the Maoist leadership of Communist China in the course of the Sino-Soviet controversy of recent years, finds a much deeper significance in the Soviet ideological changes after Stalin. It holds that they are symptoms of a degenerative process, a decline of revolutionary commitment on the part of the post-Stalin Soviet leadership, or the dominant element of it that found in Khrushchev a natural leader and spokesman. Between the Twentieth and Twenty-Second Party Congresses, it maintains, these Soviet leaders developed a complete and rounded system of revisionist views:

They put forward a revisionist line which contravenes the proletarian revolution and the dictatorship of the proletariat, a line which consists of "peaceful coexistence," "peaceful competition," "peaceful transition," "a state of the whole people," and "a party of the entire people."[5]

Hence the Soviet Union's "creative Marxism-Leninism" is in fact a species of revisionism—"Khrushchev revisionism." It expresses, and at the same time endeavors to conceal, the surreptitious departure of the Soviet ruling group from the spirit and practice of revolutionary Marxism-Leninism as taught primarily by Marx, Engels, Lenin, Stalin, and Mao Tse-tung. And Chinese communist writings have suggested that this phenomenon of Soviet deradicalization (to introduce a term of our own) goes along with, if indeed it does not grow out of, a process of *embourgeoisement* that is taking place in contemporary Soviet society, in which a new middle class has come into being, with typical middle-class aspirations for material ease and stability.

"Revisionism" is a highly charged term, signifying in the Marxist context something similar to what various religions have meant by "heresy." For descriptive and analytical purposes, we may refer to the modified Soviet ideology simply as "neocommunist Marxism." But with this reservation, and leaving aside for the moment the question of causation, I wish to suggest that the Maoist interpretation of the Soviet ideological changes may be close to the mark. The other two views unquestionably have some merit, for Soviet ideology *has* been creatively adapted to new historical circumstances and this adaptation *does* chiefly affect matters of strategy and tactics. Yet neither the Soviet official interpretation nor the dominant Western trend of thought does full justice to the phenomenon before us. The thesis of the present chapter, at any rate, is that the changes in question reflect a deradicalization of Soviet communism.

5. "The Leaders of the C.P.S.U. Are the Greatest Splitters of Our Times: Comment on the Open Letter of the Central Committee of the C.P.S.U. (VII)," *People's Daily*, Feb. 4, 1964.

Here the methodological question arises of how such a judgment might be validated. How, in other words, would one *know* whether the Soviet communist movement—or any other radical movement, communist or noncommunist—was in the stage of deradicalization? To raise this question is to focus attention upon an apparent deficiency in our theoretical apparatus. We lack a general conception of deradicalization and, in particular, of the typical symptoms of the process, the characteristic behavior of radical sociopolitical movements, including those of the Marxist persuasion, in the phase when their radicalism has subsided or is subsiding. In general, our scholarship has shown a greater interest in the rise of radical movements than in their decline. Well-known titles like *The Origins of Totalitarianism* and *The Origin of Totalitarian Democracy* reflect this bias. There is no disputing the legitimacy and fruitfulness of studying radical movements in their origins and vigorous youth. On the other hand, reflection shows that deradicalization must be the eventual fate of all radical movements, whether or not they achieve political power, and that this process too is well worth systematic analysis. Indeed, it may be that the study of such movements in the phase of deradicalization may be one avenue of deeper insight into the psychology and politics of radicalism as such.

The present study is as much or more concerned with this theoretical problem as with the particular case at hand. It seeks to conceptualize the process of deradicalization in terms of its symptoms, and thereby to suggest certain possible guidelines of analysis of recent phenomena in the development of Soviet communism. These theoretical formulations will necessarily be quite tentative and provisional, since they are derived from the study of a single historical instance of the phenomenon in question. European social democracy around the turn of the century provides an example of a Marxist movement that was indubitably in the phase of deradicalization and therefore may be a profitable case to analyze from this point of view. First, however, a few general remarks on the nature of radical movements, and on deradicalization as a stage in their development.

Radicalism: A General View

There are various ways of viewing radical politics and political movements. Some, for example, may think of radical politics as extremist politics and radical movements as those which rely upon extreme or violent methods of action. The difficulty with definitions turning on the mode of action is that extremist means are no monopoly of radical politics but are used on occasion by groups that no one would call radical.

A more promising way of arriving at a working conception of radicalism is to consider the attributes of the type of mind or outlook in which radical politics generally has its source and inspiration. Let us postulate that (1) radical social doctrines arise from time to time as expressions of the radical mind in individuals of outstanding creative power, and (2) under propitious circumstances such doctrines attract followers in significant numbers and become the ideologies of organized sociopolitical movements which may be described as radical by virtue of their being dedicated to the realization of a radical social doctrine. What, then, are the attributes of the radical mind as reflected in the type of doctrines it creates?

There is, to begin with, an intense element of negation in it. The radical is first of all someone who says "No!" to the surrounding society. He mentally and emotionally rebels against the existing order, repudiates the world as it stands, or as he perceives it to stand. For example, Marx—a quintessential example of the modern radical mind—started with a total, uncompromising denial and rejection of existing reality. Already in notes to his doctoral dissertation of 1841 he propounded this fundamental theme in the notion that "philosophy," in the persons of Hegel's disciples, was in revolt against the world. What was needed, he wrote somewhat later to his friend Arnold Ruge, was *"a merciless criticism of everything existing,* merciless in two senses: this criticism must not take fright at its own conclusions and must not shrink from a collision with the powers that be." And in his original formulation of Marxism in the *Economic and Philosophical Manuscripts of 1844,* he foretold the revolutionary transformation of this "alienated world" in which man was everywhere estranged from his own nature and being. Subsequently, his terminology changed somewhat, but his way of thought did not. World-denial is a theme running through the writings of his mature and later years as well as the early works. In a speech of 1856, as noted earlier, he pronounced sentence of capital punishment upon the bourgeois social order in the name of what he called the *Vehmgericht* or court of history, appointing the proletarian as "executioner." And for all its tortuous elaboration of abstract concepts, *Capital,* his supreme achievement, was in its way a nine-hundred-page cry of pain and outrage against bourgeois civilization as Marx perceived it.

But the radical is not adequately described as one who rejects existing reality. To understand the radical mind as found in modern Western history, we must penetrate the inner springs of its rebellion. The radical is not simply a rebel but a visionary. What inspires his rebellion against the world as it stands is his vision of an alternative universe, a *right* social order. His negation of what exists proceeds from an underlying affirmation, an idealized image of the world as it ought to be. Indeed, it is the very perfection of his alternative universe that explains the depth and totality, i.e., the *radicalness*, of his act of world-repudiation. And here again, though somewhat less obviously, Marx provides an illustration. He initially rebelled against the world in the name of the "realization of philosophy," meaning the Hegelian philosophy of man's apotheosis in history. A vision of mankind in a state of perfection was thus his starting point. As his thought developed further, realization of philosophy was redefined to mean transcendence of human self-alienation or "humanism." And humanism in this special Marxian sense was conceived as the essence of future communism, which Marx thought would come about through the socialization of private property in a world-wide proletarian revolution.

This visionary aspect of Marx's radicalism was more clearly apparent in his early writings than later on. It was superficially obscured by the attack that he and Engels made on their socialist predecessors as "utopians." In the *Communist Manifesto* and elsewhere, they derided attempts to design ideal socialist communities (such as Fourier's phalansteries) and set socialist theoreticians the task of demonstrating the necessity of capitalist society's revolutionary self-destruction. But notwithstanding their own preoccupation with this task, the founders of Marxism never lost sight of their communist utopia. The vision of a perfect communist order of the future remained integral to the Marxist social doctrine. The present bourgeois epoch represented the closing chapter of man's "prehistory," declared Marx in millenarian tones in 1859. Beyond it lay the true life of the species, when man would become fully man—a freely productive being developing his talents in all directions—in communist society. That would be humanity's great leap from the realm of necessity to the realm of freedom, wrote Engels in *Anti-Dühring*. Society, they foresaw, would become classless and conflictless with the abolition of the division of labor in all its manifold enslaving forms, and the state would disappear for lack of repressive function. Man would finally realize his own nature in a society based upon distribution according to need. Such, in broad outline, was classical Marxism's image of the ideal communist order.

One other general attribute of the radical mind remains to be mentioned: its activism. The radical not only rejects existing reality; he wants and seeks to transform it. He has not only a vision of an ideal order but a belief in the possibility of realizing it, of moving from the world as it is to the world as it ought to be. "The philosophers have only *interpreted* the world in various ways," as Marx put it in the last of his eleven theses on Feuerbach. "*The point is, to change it.*" And the radical mind, at its most creative, has a prescription for action towards this goal, a conception of revolutionary politics. In classical Marxism the prescription for action was class struggle leading to a dictatorship of the proletariat. Marx had only scorn for a socialism that would renounce the "revolutionizing of the old world" and seek, like the early Christian communities, to "achieve its salvation behind society's back."[6] He informed the proletarians that they had "a world to win," and unfurled the banner of a "revolutionary socialism" that stood for "the class dictatorship of the revolution." This was to be achieved, finally, by proletarian upheavals in a number of leading countries bringing the overthrow of bourgeois rule and the seizure and socialization of the means of production.

A full statement of the conditions under which radical movements arise in society is more than can be attempted here. But, paraphrasing Lenin in *What Is To Be Done?*, we can say without much exaggeration that there can be no radical movement without a radical social doctrine to serve as its inspiration and ideology. The movement develops as an institutionalization of the radical doctrine, as the orga-

6. *The Eighteenth Brumaire*, p. 21.

nized activity of a group (party, association, etc.) dedicated to the realization of the vision of a new society. By the nature of the self-selective process of initial recruitment, the movement's leadership, which may originally include the author or authors of the radical creed, will consist in large part of persons attracted to the doctrine by their own radical tendency of mind. On the other hand, some may be persons chiefly gifted in practical organizing ability. If conditions are propitious, as in a time of widespread misery and discontent, the movement may attract followers in large enough numbers to turn into a genuine mass movement. But many in the mass following may join the movement for motives other than zeal for the radical cause. Cases in point would be radical socialist movements with a mass membership arising out of their association with trade unions.

It appears to be the fate of radical movements that survive and flourish for long *without* remaking the world that they undergo eventually a process of deradicalization. A loss of *élan* is not necessarily involved, for this process can go on in a movement at a time of significant growth and advance. Deradicalization signifies a subtle change in the movement's relation to the social milieu. Essentially, it settles down and adjusts itself to existence within the very order that it officially desires to overthrow and transform. This is not to say that the movement turns into a conservative social force opposed to social change. Rather, it becomes "reformist" in the sense that it accepts the established system and its institutionalized procedures as the framework for further efforts in the direction of social change. A resolution adopted by the Congress of Parties of the Second International at Amsterdam in August 1904 conveys a vivid sense of this process in a passage warning against it:

The Congress condemns in the most decisive fashion revisionist efforts to change the victorious tactics we have hitherto followed based on the class struggle, in such a way that instead of conquering political power by defeating our opponents, a policy of coming to terms with the existing order is followed. The result of such revisionist tactics would be that instead of being a party which works for the most rapid transformation possible of existing bourgeois society into the socialist order, i.e., revolutionary in the best sense of the word, the party would become one which is content with reforming bourgeois society.[7]

The phrase "coming to terms with the existing order" best indicates what deradicalization means. In the stage of deradicalization, the movement loses its revolutionary otherworldliness, the alienation from existing conditions arising out of its commitment to a future perfect order, and makes an accommodation to the world as it stands.

Among the numerous and complex causal factors in deradicalization, two are particularly noteworthy: leadership change and worldly success. So far as the first is concerned, it is clear that mere continued official adherence to a radical social doctrine cannot preserve radicalism in a movement if the leadership, through aging or change of leaders, ceases to be radical in its outlook. The radical tendency of mind, as suggested above, is likely to be dominant among the original generation of the movement's leaders. In the normal course of events, however, this situation will eventually change. Not only may some among the original generation of leaders mellow as they grow older, but younger persons who rise through the movement into leadership positions are less likely than the original leaders to be radical types. Am-

7. Quoted in James Joll, *The Second International 1889–1914* (London: Weidenfeld and Nicolson, 1955), pp. 101–102.

bition, organizing ability, and concern for the interests of the organization and its social constituency are likely to be their predominant characteristics. Successive generations of leaders will show less and less of the alienation from the existing order that characterized the radical founders of the movement and their associates.

Turning to the second factor, there seems to be an inverse relationship between a radical movement's organizational strength and the preservation of its radicalism. Radical movements that remain small sectarian groups on the fringe of society are relatively impervious to deradicalization; the history of twentieth-century Trotskyism furnishes numerous illustrations. But when a radical movement grows large and strong, acquires a big organizational structure, a mass social constituency, and a recognized place in society, this very worldly success fosters deradicalization. The acquisition of a mass membership inevitably dilutes the movement's radicalism, and the influence of the relatively less radical rank-and-file will make itself felt in various ways at the leadership level. Moreover, when society begins to accord a measure of acceptance to a radical movement, this may tend to weaken, if not eventually dissipate, the sharp sense of alienation from this world and the commitment to a future order which characterized the movement in its earlier phases. Above all, a movement that grows strong and influential and has prospects of further growth acquires a definite stake in the stability of the order in which this success has been won—a stake that is no less real for the fact that it goes unacknowledged. Robert Michels stressed this point in his study of socialist parties. Observing that the revolutionary political party is at first a state within the state, pursuing the avowed aim of supplanting the present social order with a new one, Michels argued that the growth of the party as an organization weakens the commitment to the revolutionary aim. For revolutionary action can only endanger the position of a party that has achieved a mass membership, a bureaucracy, a full treasury, and a network of financial and moral interests extending all over the country. So it is that "from a means, organization becomes an end" and that "the party grows increasingly inert as the strength of its organization grows; it loses its revolutionary impetus, becomes sluggish. . . ."[8]

Deradicalization of Social Democratic Parties

Michels' thoughts on the deradicalization of revolutionary political parties were generalizations from the observed experience of European Marxist parties in the late nineteenth and early twentieth centuries, the German Social Democratic Party (SPD) in particular .The 1880's had witnessed the emergence in various Western European countries of mass working-class parties professing revolutionary Marxism as their ideology. The largest and most influential was the SPD, which in 1875 had become a united body under the leadership of Wilhelm Liebknecht and August Bebel and with Marx and Engels as its mentors and advisers. Notwithstanding the harassment and repression endured under Bismarck's Anti-Socialist Law of 1878–1890, the SPD waxed strong in late nineteenth-century Germany. In the elections of 1890, it received nearly a million and a half votes—about a fifth of those cast—and thirty-five seats in the Reichstag. Thirteen years later, a remarkable electoral victory gave the party over three million votes and eighty-one Reichstag seats. And by the elections of 1912, its membership totalled nearly a million and its electoral strength exceeded four

8. Michels, *Political Parties* (New York: Dover Publications, 1959), pp. 370, 371, 372–373.

million votes, making the SPD both the largest party in Germany and the largest socialist party in the world.

In the aftermath of persecution under the Anti-Socialist Law, the party firmly restated its radical goals and principles in the new program adopted at its Erfurt Congress in 1891. Yet by the turn of the century if not earlier, this formidable mass Marxist party and the movement over which it presided were far along in the process of deradicalization. Marx and Engels were now dead, and a second generation of leaders, typified by Eduard Bernstein and the party theorist Karl Kautsky, had come to the fore. The party's radical orientation was tempered by its association with a decidedly unradical trade-union movement whose tendency was to work toward piecemeal economic reform. And deradicalization was fostered by the great growth of the movement —its wealth, organizational strength, widespread influence, and seeming prospects for further gradual increase of power under the prevailing social system.

It is beyond question that around the turn of the century the German and other European social democratic movements were settling down and coming to terms with the existing order. But what were the symptoms of this process? In what ways did the movements reflect and react to it? The principal manifestations of deradicalization were of four different kinds, having to do with the action-pattern of the movement, its relation to its ideological goals, the development of its strategy and tactics, and, finally, its inner conflicts. Taking the German Marxist movement as a classic case, let us now examine these points.

The accommodation with the existing system was shown first of all in the emergence of a reformist, as distinguished from a revolutionary, pattern of action. The movement's political action lost all meaningful orientation toward the coming great upheaval foretold in the Marxist ideology, and concentrated more and more on what was called the *Gegen-*

wartsarbeit, or everyday work, of the party. The electoral activity of the party expanded with its electoral success. "Everywhere there is action for reform, action for social progress, action for the victory of democracy," wrote Eduard Bernstein in the famous articles in *Neue Zeit* that proved the manifesto of Marxist revisionism. "People study the details of the problems of the day and seek for levers and starting points to carry on the development of society in the direction of socialism." It would therefore be better, he argued, if social democracy "could find the courage to emancipate itself from a phraseology which is actually outworn and if it would make up its mind to appear what it is in reality today: a democratic socialistic party of reform."[9]

But that is precisely what the party, or rather its dominant, so-called "orthodox," faction refused to do. It reasserted its ideological revolutionism at the very time when its practical reformism was becoming most pronounced. In the Erfurt Program, as mentioned above, the party had reaffirmed its radical mission as a revolutionary anti-capitalist organization destined to unite and lead the working class in what was described as an ever more bitter class war between bourgeoisie and proletariat. And this in essence remained the party's line in the aftermath of appeals by Georg von Vollmar, Bernstein, and other influential Social Democrats for abandonment of the Marxist theory of catastrophe and the gospel of revolution through class war. Not only did Kautsky at the turn of the century defend the radical goals and principles of the movement in response to Bernstein's critique, but the party formally condemned the latter at its Hanover Congress in 1899 and again at the Dresden Congress of 1903. Furthermore, the Dresden Congress' resolution on this point was adopted by the Socialist Inter-

9. Eduard Bernstein, *Evolutionary Socialism,* pp. 197, 199.

national at its Amsterdam Congress the following year and thus was made binding upon all member parties. And right up to the eve of 1914, when the German party's support for war credits in the Reichstag demonstrated conclusively how far it had done in deradicalization, it officially continued to regard itself as utterly alienated from bourgeois society. "Social Democracy differs from all other parties through its fundamental opposition to the social and governmental system of capitalism," declared the report of the Parliamentary Party to the SPD Congress in 1912.[10]

So it was that a deradicalized social democratic movement pledged its allegiance anew to ideological orthodoxy while adhering in practice to a reformist policy line. Instead of abandoning its radical principles and aims in accordance with the revisionist program, the party renewed and even intensified its formal commitment to these aims and principles. Why the dominant element of the leadership moved in this direction was hinted in a letter from an elder German Socialist, Ignaz Auer, to Bernstein.

> Do you think it is really possible that a party which has a literature going back fifty years, an organization going back forty years and a still older tradition, can change its direction like this in the twinkling of an eye? [he inquired.] For the most influential members of the party to behave as you demand would simply mean splitting the party and throwing decades of work to the winds. My dear Ede, one doesn't formally decide to do what you ask, one doesn't say it, one *does* it.[11]

This was to say that the party's interests militated against any tampering with its ideological *raison d'etre.* To preserve the unity and stability of the movement, its leaders had to show great care and restraint in their capacity as custodians

10. Quoted in Joll, p. 90.
11. *Ibid.,* pp. 93–94.

of its revolutionary ideology. Similar reasoning underlay the resistance of Austrian social democratic leaders like Victor Adler to demands raised in the movement in the 1890's for a theoretical reappraisal of some fundamental concepts of orthodox Marxism which were not being vindicated by contemporary economic development. Such demands, we are told, were "strenuously resisted by Adler, not so much on ideological grounds, for he was anything but a doctrinaire Marxist, but rather for fear of provoking dissensions which might once more endanger party unity."[12]

All this suggests that the process of deradicalization has a certain inner "dialectic." For deep-seated reasons, theory and practice diverge. The movement intensifies its theoretical adherence to revolutionary goals at the very time when in practice it moves down the path of reformism. The dominant leadership resists the counsel of the Bernsteins who want the radical theory to be revised to accord with the reformist practice and follows the contrary counsel of those who argue that "one doesn't say it, one *does* it." Far from succumbing to doctrinal revisionism, it resoundingly reaffirms its official revolutionism and pledges its allegiance anew to its original radical outlook. And it does so, at least in part, in an effort to preserve the movement's integrity, to prevent or lessen the demoralization and disunity that open avowal of reformism would tend to provoke. As we shall note presently, it may also be impelled in this direction by accusations from strongly radical elements within the movement that it is betraying the revolutionary cause.

The appearance of a serious discrepancy between revolutionism in theory and reformism in practice is thus one of the hallmarks of deradicalization. But for subjective reasons as well as vulnerability to accusations of hypocrisy from within the movement, the leadership is uncomfortable

12. Norbert Leser, "Austro-Marxism: A Reappraisal," *Journal of Contemporary History*, I, 2 (1966), p. 118.

in the presence of this discrepancy and does what it can to lessen or blur it. While rejecting the formal revisionism that would disavow the radical principles or eschatological elements of the movement's ideology, the orthodox leaders modify the *tactical* part of the ideology by stressing immediate short-term objectives and nonradical means of attaining them. And in their exegeses of the authoritative writings and pronouncements of the founders, they highlight those statements that give (or seem to give) sanction to such a development of the tactical doctrine. This, at any rate, was the road taken by the social democratic leaders.

What had come to be called the "minimum program" of the movement, embracing lesser goals attainable without revolutionizing the existing order, was emphasized at the expense of the truly revolutionary "maximum program," but on the official assumption that every step in fulfillment of the movement's minimal program would likewise bring closer the realization of the maximal program. The democratic electoral road to power was increasingly treated as the highroad, and a doctrine of socialist "parliamentarianism" arose. Thus in his commentary on the Erfurt Program, Kautsky reproved the early "proletarian utopians" like Wilhelm Weitling for having viewed as a betrayal of the movement "every form of the class struggle which was not aimed at the immediate overthrow of the existing order, that is, every serious, efficient sort of effort. . . ."[13] Again, in lectures delivered before an Amsterdam socialist group in 1902, he extolled democracy as "light and air to the proletariat." Elections were "a means to count ourselves and the enemy," and further:

They prevent premature outbreaks and they guard against defeats. They also grant the possibility that the

13. Karl Kautsky, *The Class Struggle* (*Erfurt Program*) (Chicago: Charles H. Kerr, 1910), pp. 196, 197.

opponents will themselves recognize the untenability of many positions and freely surrender them when their maintenance is no life-and-death question for them.

Kautsky

He foresaw that parliamentarianism, in decline under capitalism, would be "reawakened to new youth and strength when it, together with the total governmental power, is conquered by the rising proletariat and turned to serve its purposes." And how would the governmental power be conquered by the proletariat? Not by an armed uprising, Kautsky cautioned, save possibly in Russia. Unlike some past revolutions, the coming revolution would be a long-drawn-out political "civil war" without battles, barricades, and blood, i.e., a figurative civil war. It would not, moreover, be a "battle of mobs," but rather: "It is a battle of organized, intelligent masses, full of stability and prudence, that do not follow every impulse or explode over every insult, or collapse under every misfortune."[14]

In keeping with this concept, orthodox Marxists gave an exegesis of the Marxist scriptures which laid particular emphasis upon everything that pointed toward a well-behaved class struggle. It is questionable whether Marx and Engels (particularly Marx) ever wavered in their commitment to the radical *Weltanschauung* that they formulated as young men. But in their later years, owing in part to involvement in the intricate politics of the revolutionary movement, they made various statements that seemed to sanction gradualism, an electoral orientation, and a belief in a peaceful path of

14. Kautsky, *The Social Revolution*, pp. 79–82, 88. All this bears out the comment of Alfred Meyer that "Kautsky still spoke about the proletarian revolution but demanded that it be a tame and civilized revolution" (*Marxism: The Unity of Theory and Practice* [Ann Arbor: University of Michigan Press, 1953], p. 135). A detailed and useful discussion of trends in social democratic Marxism at the end of the nineteenth century is contained in chapters 5 and 6 of this book.

socialist revolution. Thus Marx's inaugural address to the International Workingmen's Association in 1864 welcomed the ten-hour day as a victory for the "political economy of labor," suggesting that more such reforms within the capitalist order represented a real path of progress to socialism. In a speech at Amsterdam in 1872, after a congress of the International, he allowed that in countries like England and America, and possibly Holland as well, the worker might be able to attain his goal by peaceful means. Engels too referred to the possibility of a peaceful revolution in his critique of the Erfurt Program. More important still, in his 1895 preface to a new edition of Marx's *Class Struggles in France*, Engels gave his blessing to the parliamentary mode of struggle by hailing the German social democracy's two million voters as the decisive "shock force" of the international proletarian army. "The irony of world history turns everything upside down," he went on. "We, the 'revolutionaries,' the 'rebels'—we are thriving far better on legal methods than on illegal methods and revolt. The parties of order, as they call themselves, are perishing under the legal conditions created by themselves."[15]

These and like texts proved of great importance to the leadership of a movement in which all policy had to be legitimated by reference to authoritative pronouncements of the founders of the ideology. Having undertaken to paper over the discrepancy between its theoretical revolu-

15. Preface to Marx, *The Class Struggles in France*, pp. 27, 28. Michels suggests that this influential endorsement by Engels of parliamentary methods for attaining socialism did not give expression to his true opinions. In this connection he quotes from a letter that Engels wrote to Kautsky saying, with reference to the preface: "My text had to suffer from the timid legalism of our friends in Berlin, who dreaded a second edition of the anti-socialist laws—a dread to which I was forced to pay attention at the existing political juncture." Michels concludes on this basis that "Engels would seem to have been the victim of an opportunist sacrifice of principles to the needs of organization, a sacrifice made for love of the party and in opposition to his known theoretical convictions" (*Political Parties*, p. 370 n.).

tionism and practical reformism by prescribing gradualist and peaceful *tactics* of revolutionary struggle, social democratic Marxism naturally gave special attention and emphasis to such statements by Marx and Engels as those just cited. By the same token, it tended to de-emphasize the many Marx-Engels texts which visualized the socialist revolution as the forcible overthrow of all existing conditions by "illegal methods and revolt" and which visualized the regime of the revolution as a violent dictatorship of the proletariat. Thus a definite line in the exegesis of classical Marxism was part of the general process of deradicalization of the social democratic Marxist movement. A sort of retrospective deradicalization of the radical godfathers of the movement, Marx and Engels, was one of its manifestations.

So, finally, was conflict in the movement between the orthodox leadership and elements whose radical alienation from the existing order and commitment to the revolutionary vision of a new world remained unimpaired by the movement's worldly success. Reflection shows that such conflict is virtually inescapable when a movement is in the stage of deradicalization, so much so that the absence of it may be treated as a sure sign that no fundamental deradicalization is taking place. What explains this fact is that the leadership (not to mention the rank-and-file) of a radical movement is never homogeneous in outlook. There are bound to be differences of temperament, of relationship to the ideology, of position in the movement. For reasons touched on above, some of the more adaptable leaders will preside over the movement's deradicalization. But other, more consistently radical-minded elements will rebel against this process, and here lie the seeds of inner conflict or even schism in the movement.

Seeing the discrepancy between the officially-avowed revolutionary theory and the unrevolutionary day-to-day practice, the genuine radicals will be profoundly worried by the direction the movement is taking. "What is happening," they will ask. Are we not giving up in practice our cherished goals, our effort to transform society totally? Is not the movement drifting into opportunism? Are we not, then, betraying the founders of the doctrine in whose name we continue to speak? Among the prominent figures in the social democratic movement who raised such troubled and troublesome questions were Rosa Luxemburg, Anton Pannekoek, and Wilhelm Liebknecht's son Karl, of whom it has been said that he inherited his father's political romanticism without his common sense.[16] Like revisionists of the Bernsteinian persuasion, the genuine radicals craved consistency. But the two groups moved in opposite directions in search of it. Whereas the revisionists wanted to revise the revolutionary theory to accord with reformist practice, the radicals wanted to abandon reformist practice out of fidelity to the revolutionary world-image; they took the movement's eschatology seriously.

The inner conflict attendant upon a movement's deradicalization may be all the more deep and disruptive if it is an international movement, as Marxist social democracy was in the early years of this century. For heterogeneity of outlook among the leaders is even more to be expected on an international scale than within a given national branch of the movement. One reason for this is that at any given time the movement may be in different stages of development in various countries. This may result in the ascendancy of a group of one outlook in one branch of the international movement, and of a group of opposed outlook in another. In that event, a schism may occur, as it did in the international Marxist movement in 1917 and after. German ortho-

16. Joll, p. 100. On the radicals' rebellion against the tendency of deradicalization, see Meyer, pp. 136–139. He writes of Rosa Luxemburg, in particular, that "her entire political life was one momentous attempt to reunite the theory and practice of Marxian socialism in the radical spirit of its founders" (p. 137).

dox Marxism had a counterpart in the Menshevik wing of the younger Russian social democracy. But the Marxism that came to power in Russia in the October Revolution of 1917 was the radical Bolshevik Marxism of Lenin and his associates. The international Marxist movement was consequently split in two, and soon a deradicalized social democracy with its center of gravity in Western Europe found itself in hostile confrontation with a radical Marxist movement of Leninist persuasion centering in Soviet Russia and laying undivided claim to the Marxist heritage.

Radicalism and Deradicalization
Under Lenin and Stalin

It is always risky to interpret a massive historical event in terms of a single cause or issue. But it seems undeniable that rebellious protest against the deradicalization of social democracy was a central motif in the great Marxist schism and in the rise of communist Marxism as a new world-wide movement. The younger Lenin had venerated Kautsky as a Marxist teacher and adversary of revisionism. But during the World War, in which Kautsky and many other European social democratic leaders failed to oppose the warring governments in the name of the previously espoused principle of international working-class solidarity, Lenin turned against them. In a pamphlet published in Geneva in 1915, he accused Kautsky of paying mere "lip service" to Marxism. Speaking of the Kautskys of the international social democratic movement, he went on:

> Those people castrate Marxism; they purge it, by means of obvious sophisms, of its revolutionary living soul; they recognize in Marxism *everything except*

revolutionary means of struggle, except the advocacy of, and the preparation for, such struggle, and the education of the masses in this direction.[17]

In 1917, on the eve of taking power, Lenin insisted on changing the name of his party from "Social Democratic" to "Communist" in order to sharpen symbolically his break with social democratic Marxism. The subsequent creation of the Third International was a logical outgrowth of this step.

Leninist or communist Marxism emerged as a kind of Marxist fundamentalism, a revival of the radical essence of Marx's thought. On the opening page of *The State and Revolution*—one of the great documents of Marxist radicalism—Lenin declared that the pressing need was to restore to Marxism its revolutionary soul and thus combat the efforts of vulgarizers like Kautsky to omit, obliterate, and distort the revolutionary side of the doctrine. Here and in other writings of this period, he hammered out the foundations of communist Marxism in a savage polemic against Kautskyan social democracy and its interpretation of Marx and Engels. Kautsky, he contended, was guilty of "petty-bourgeois distortion of Marxism and base renunciation of it *in practice*, while hypocritically recognizing it *in words*."[18] The essence of Kautskyism, as Lenin saw it, was, in our terms, the discrepancy between revolutionary theory and nonrevolutionary practice which shows up when a movement undergoes deradicalization.

Kautsky's exegesis of the Marx-Engels texts was a particular target of Lenin's polemic. "How Kautsky Transformed Marx into a Common or Garden Liberal" was the title of the opening section of *The Proletarian Revolution and the Renegade Kautsky*. And Lenin argued in this and other

17. *Selected Works*, II, 359.
18. Lenin, *The State and Revolution*, in *Selected Works*, II, 163.

writings of the period for a fundamentalist reading of the views of Marx and Engels on revolution and dictatorship. To be a true Marxist, one had not only to accept the class struggle but also the proletarian dictatorship as its culmination and the necessary way station to the new world of communist society. A proletarian revolution meant the taking of power by an armed uprising; and Marx, were he alive now, would no longer allow for the possibility of a peaceful path to socialism in Britain and America, since the exceptional conditions that might have made peaceful revolution possible there in the nineteenth century no longer obtained. And the dictatorship of the proletariat—the theory of which constituted the very essence of Marxist teaching—was a revolutionary regime relying upon force and violence to suppress its class enemies.

Thus communist Marxism took shape as the political doctrine of a new anti-social democratic Marxist radicalism. Now, nearly a half-century after Lenin, the Soviet communist movement still claims to be authentically "Marxist-Leninist." But if deradicalization, as suggested above, is the general fate of radical movements, the question arises whether this fate has been overtaking Soviet communism in the recent past. One way of approaching it may be to inquire whether Soviet communism has begun to show such symptoms of deradicalization as those displayed in its time by the social democratic movement. Such comparative treatment seems logically feasible despite the fact that in the one case we are dealing with a radical movement that came to power, while the other movement remained out of power.

It could be argued that Soviet communism entered upon the phase of deradicalization long before Stalin's death. There were, for example, indications of deradicalization as early as the period of the New Economic Policy in the 1920's, most notably in the regime's action-pattern in both international and domestic affairs. True, the revival of revolutionary militance at the close of the 1920's, both internally and to some extent externally, points to the inconclusiveness of those earlier signs. Soviet foreign policy in the Popular Front period of the middle 1930's, however, could again be seen as symptomatic of deradicalization—and some in the West so saw it. Moreover, two of the factors in deradicalization that have been emphasized in these pages—change in the composition of the leadership and the worldly success that gives a one-time radical movement a stake in the existing order—were evident, or becoming so, as the Bolshevik old guard began to be replaced by a new generation of Soviet leaders. It might be mentioned, too, that the charge of deradicalization—couched in such terms as "bureaucratic degeneration" and "Thermidor"—bulked large in the Trotskyist polemic against Stalinist Soviet communism. It was, in particular, Trotsky's fundamental thesis in *The Revolution Betrayed* (1937) that Soviet communism, despite continued lip-service to revolutionary Marxism, had undergone a far-reaching deradicalization under the aegis of a basically conservative bureaucracy of which Stalin himself was the personification. The Great Purge of the middle 1930's and Stalin's super-cautious foreign policy of that time appeared to Trotsky, along with much else, as evidence in support of this thesis. The Great Purge, in which most of the still-surviving old Bolshevik revolutionaries perished or were sent once more to Siberia, was seen as a counterrevolution of conservatism.

There is no denying that Stalinist Soviet communism showed conservative features, particularly in its later years. But apart from the fact (or in connection with it) that Stalin himself was fundamentally misconstrued as a mere personification of the Soviet bureaucracy, there were deep flaws in the Trotskyist analysis. Although the Soviet communist movement undoubtedly underwent very considerable deradicalization during the Stalin era, Stalin himself, a man of the original revolutionary generation, represented in his peculiar way a link with the radical Leninist past and a bar to *full-scale* development of the deradicalizing tendencies that had become strong in Soviet communism. In internal policy, for example, he espoused in his *Economic Problems of Socialism in the U.S.S.R.* (1952) the idea that the Soviet agrarian economy should soon begin to be based not on monetary relationships but on direct "product-exchange"; and this radical prescription, along with his projection of a policy of economic austerity for the Soviet Union in its further advance towards "full communism," may help to explain why, in subsequent years of Soviet de-Stalinization, the Chinese communist leader Mao Tse-tung has defended Stalin as a great Marxist-Leninist mentor for communist movements.

In foreign policy, moreover, Stalin demonstrated his surviving—or reviving—commitment to Marxist revolutionism by presiding over a largely forcible expansion of the communist system to other countries after the end of the Second World War. And whatever the mixture of motives actuating him, it is notable that an analysis of his action widely accepted in the West saw it as deriving from continued acceptance of radical Marxist-Leninist goals.[19] It is true that Stalin's postwar revolutionism had its limits. Possibly fearing great-power competition from within the international communist movement, he did not, for example, show initial enthusiasm for a communist takeover of China. It is likewise true that Stalin acted with a certain circumspection and caution in the process of exporting communism to other countries. This is understandable when we consider that the age of atomic weapons had dawned and that Russia was not only without them but also weakened by the ordeal of war. But caution in the pursuit of radical ends is no derogation of radicalism itself. To this it should

19. I refer to the analysis by George F. Kennan in his influential article on "The Sources of Soviet Conduct" in *Foreign Affairs* (July, 1947).

be added that so long as Stalin lived, there was no serious departure from the strategic and tactical fundamentals of the Marxist-Leninist doctrine of world revolution as codified in the 1920's and 1930's under Stalin's aegis. This fact is all the more significant in the light of available evidence, to which I shall refer presently, that Stalin in the last years of his life was strenuously resisting some doctrinal changes which were being advocated by other Soviet political leaders and which would have been indicative of Soviet deradicalization.

Soviet Deradicalization Since Stalin

The real question, then, is not whether Soviet communism began to deradicalize before Stalin died, although there are strong indications that it did. Rather, the question is whether the deradicalizing tendency already apparent in earlier years but always held in check may have come to much fuller fruition in the post-Stalin period, whether the passing of Stalin and the consequent emergence of a new generation of Soviet leaders has brought the Soviet communist movement into a highly advanced or even final phase of deradicalization. In short, is Soviet communism of the late 1950's and middle 1960's to be seen as a basically deradicalized Marxist movement? If we can take the symptoms that were shown by the social democratic Marxist movement in its phase of deradicalization as criteria for judgment, an affirmative answer is indicated.

We see, to begin with, a coming to terms with the existing order, both internationally and internally, in the action-pattern of the Soviet communist leadership. In Soviet foreign relations there have, it is true, been episodes in which force was egregiously employed or serious risks incurred; the Hungarian intervention of 1956, the Cuban missiles venture of 1962, and the invasion of Czechoslovakia in 1968 are obvious cases in point. Yet none of these Soviet actions is necessarily to be interpreted as the action of a revolutionary power intent upon altering the international sociopolitical status quo.[20] The Czech intervention, in particular, was a classic act of counterrevolution, and very reminiscent of Tsarist Russia's behavior in the nineteenth century. And the general pattern of Soviet international conduct in the post-Stalin period has been distinctly unrevolutionary. The Soviet regime has sought a *rapprochement* with noncommunist nationalist regimes in the underdeveloped areas of the world. In certain critical junctures in international affairs, it has found it possible to support noncommunist India engaged in conflict with Communist China. It has attempted to mediate a dispute between noncommunist India and noncommunist Pakistan. It has shown a desire to settle the war in Vietnam, even at the expense of full (or early) realization of communist aims in South Vietnam. In addition to all this, it has intermittently sought to improve relations and institutionalize a measure of cooperation with the leading noncommunist power of the West. In internal policy, moreover, the Soviet regime has increasingly turned away from doctrinaire schemes toward a more pragmatic policy line in the economic and other spheres. The recent experimentation with market principles in the economy is only one of many expressions of this.

20. In the Hungarian intervention, the Soviet motivation was probably mainly defensive, since the preservation of the Soviet position in Eastern Europe was threatened by Hungarian departure from the Warsaw Alliance. In the Cuban missiles episode, the Soviet aim seems to have been to redress an adverse balance of nuclear power in a comparatively inexpensive way. And the Soviet aggression against Czechoslovakia in 1968 is properly to be seen as the counterrevolutionary action of a government frightened by the spectre of liberalized communism. It is more to be compared with the nineteenth-century European interventions of the openly counterrevolutionary Tsarist Russian government than with the international actions (e.g., the Polish campaign of 1920) undertaken by Russian communism when it was still a revolutionary political force.

But the "dialectic" of deradicalization, too, seems to have been operative in the post-Stalin period. The tendency of the regime to adjust its conduct at home and abroad to existing situations and realities has been accompanied by no diminution of ideological rhetoric. On the contrary, verbal protestations of fidelity to communist ideas have intensified, and there has been something of a Leninist revival in Soviet propaganda. Frequently, and in the strongest terms, the leadership has reaffirmed its dedication to the final goals of communism as laid down by Marx, Engels, and Lenin. It has insisted, as mentioned earlier, that peaceful coexistence can never embrace "ideological coexistence," i.e., that the ideological gulf between communist and noncommunist societies remains unbridged and unbridgeable. It was, moreover, in this very period that a Soviet leader issued the warning that Soviet communists would not renounce their communist principles until "the shrimps whistle" and flung down the gauntlet to capitalist America in the famous phrase: "We will bury you!" The image of the future communist social order reappeared in shining form in Khrushchev's address to the Twenty-First Party Congress in 1959 and again in the new Party Program in 1961; and never in Soviet history was so much official public attention bestowed upon the utopian vision of the communist future. It is symptomatic that the new Party Program envisages, with the advent of a full communist society in Russia some time after 1980, the radical transformation of Soviet man himself into "a new man who will . . . combine spiritual wealth, moral purity, and a perfect physique."[21]

---

21. Mendel, *Essential Works of Marxism,* p. 468. It may be noted that Khrushchev's phrase, "We will bury you!," was widely misunderstood abroad. In colloquial Russian, the words carry the meaning: "We will be present at your funeral," i.e., we will outlive you. The flamboyant statement was not, then, a threat to destroy but rather a boast that Soviet communism would outlive the noncommunist system in the long-range competition of systems that Khrushchev called "peaceful coexistence."

The pledging of allegiance anew to communism's eschatology has, however, been accompanied by the third symptom of deradicalization—revision of the tactical doctrine, changes in the official conception of the *means* by which the ultimate goals may be achieved. As noted earlier, these changes center in the general idea that communism can spread in the world by peaceful means, without "export of revolution" (i.e., the use of armed force to impose communist revolutions from without) or internal civil war. In elaborating the programmatic notion of a peaceful path to communism, Soviet sources have put forward a new doctrine of parliamentarianism which strikingly parallels the above-mentioned Kautskyan picture of a takeover of power through the winning of a parliamentary majority by the working class. In keeping with this same trend of thought, Soviet official writings have endorsed the essentially gradualist tactic (originally developed by the Italian communist leader Palmiro Togliatti) of communist advocacy of economic "structural reforms" within the frame of the existing order. And on the broader plane of general strategy, Soviet doctrine has broken with the Leninist thesis on the inevitability of wars and espoused, as we saw, the view that the Soviet Union can best contribute to the further spread of communism by winning the battle of economic development in peaceful competitive coexistence.

These doctrinal developments have been accompanied by appropriate adjustments in the official Soviet image of the movement's founders. To some extent, in fact, we see a retrospective "deradicalization" of the Marxist-Leninist classics. Thus the 1961 Party Program, in elaborating upon the theme of parliamentary transition to socialism, ascribes to Marx and Lenin the view that it may prove possible to buy out the bourgeoisie:

It may well be that . . . there will arise in certain countries a situation in which it will be preferable for the bourgeoisie, as Marx and Lenin foresaw it, to agree to the means of production being purchased from it and for the proletariat to "pay off" the bourgeoisie.[22]

Lenin is said to have granted (and by implication to have preferred) the possibility that the Russian revolution would develop peacefully.[23] And great emphasis is placed upon an obscure Lenin statement to the effect that "we exert our chief influence upon the international revolution through our economic policy."[24] Thus, neocommunist Marxism is projected back upon the radical founders of the movement, including Lenin.

The fourth mark of deradicalization—conflict in the movement between those who take the lead in this process and those who resist it—has also been present. The rise of neocommunist Marxism in the Soviet Union was not a smooth and painless development reflecting a consensus of the communist leadership. These doctrinal changes were the subject of an intense and bitter debate that began while Stalin was still alive. Irrefutable evidence on this point is contained in his final published work, *Economic Problems of Socialism in the U.S.S.R.*, a record of Stalin's interventions in a discussion carried on inside the Soviet regime in 1951–1952 in preparation for the Nineteenth Party Congress. There he took issue with unnamed "comrades" who were contending that Lenin's thesis on the inevitability of wars under imperialism was obsolete and in need of revision, and that such wars had ceased to be inevitable. In other words, the new doctrine on non-inevitability, which was first promulgated at the Twentieth Party Congress in 1956, *had been advocated behind the scenes in Stalin's final years.* But Stalin would have none of it.

22. Mendel, p. 402.
23. See, for example, Khrushchev's public speech to the Twentieth Party Congress, *Pravda*, Feb. 15, 1956.
24. I. Inozemtsev, "Leninizm—nauchnaia osnova sovetskoi vneshnei politiki," *Kommunist*, No. 7 (1966), p. 23.

"These comrades are mistaken," he declared. "To eliminate the inevitability of war, it is necessary to abolish imperialism."[25] Since, in other words, wars would remain inevitable so long as the world communist revolution remained
basically incomplete, the only road to peace was the round-
about road of forcible communist revolution, with all that
this implied for further growth of international tension. The
call to moderate communist tactics implicit in the thesis on
the noninevitability of wars in our time was thus rejected.
This obdurate defense by Stalin of Marxist-Leninist ideological orthodoxy was indirectly a demand for indefinite
prolongation of the cold war pending the spread of communist revolution to other countries. It was of a piece, moreover, with his concluding speech at the Nineteenth Party
Congress in October 1952. In what was to prove his vale-
dictory, Stalin applauded the continuing progress of the
world communist revolution and set the course of the movement towards its further advance in the coming years. In
the light of this and other evidence, it is impossible to accept
the view of some Western scholars that Stalin in the final
period of his life was preparing the realignment of Soviet
foreign policy which took place after his death.[26] On the
contrary, he was engaged in a determined struggle against
change, against forces within his own regime that were
pressing for an international *détente* and realignment of
policy.

Stalin's death removed the most formidable opponent of
the revision of the Leninist thesis on inevitability of wars
and related doctrinal as well as policy changes. But "heirs
of Stalin" remained strong within the Soviet leadership, and

25. *Economic Problems of Socialism in the U.S.S.R.*, pp. 27–28, 30.
26. See, for example, Marshall D. Shulman, *Stalin's Foreign Policy Re-
appraised* (Cambridge, Mass.: Harvard University Press, 1963). For a
fuller presentation of the evidence *against* the view that Stalin was preparing a realignment of foreign policy in his final period, see *The Soviet
Political Mind*, ch. 2.

post-Stalin ideological change was contested. As late as October 1961, on the eve of the Twenty-Second Party Congress, Vyacheslav Molotov addressed a letter to the Party Central Committee protesting against the doctrinal revisions in the draft Party Program scheduled for adoption by the Congress; and the storm of abuse he thereby brought down upon himself at the Congress suggests that his message struck a sensitive chord in many Soviet communist minds. By this time, however, the conflict over the post-Stalin trend of development in Soviet communism had been internationalized. Resistance to this trend from within the international communist movement had found a powerful and vigorous champion in the Maoist leadership of the Chinese Communist party.

Soviet sources have asserted that the great Sino-Soviet ideological dispute began in April, 1960, when the Chinese communist press published, on the occasion of the ninetieth anniversary of Lenin's birth, a series of implicitly polemical articles entitled "Long Live Leninism!" Chinese communist sources have contested this, pointing out that "It takes more than a cold day for the river to freeze three feet deep." The real starting point, according to the Chinese view, was the Twentieth Party Congress: "Ever since the Twentieth Congress of the C.P.S.U., we have watched with concern as the C.P.S.U. leadership took the road of revisionism." To substantiate this claim, the Chinese have revealed that in April 1956, shortly after the adoption of an anti-Stalin line by the Twentieth Congress, Mao Tse-tung emphasized to Mikoyan and the Soviet Ambassador in China that Stalin's "merits outweigh his faults." Repeatedly in subsequent months, the Chinese leaders, in private conversations with Soviet officials, opposed the anti-Stalin line. And in November 1957, when a conference of communist leaders from all over the world took place in Moscow to formulate the international communist line, conflict broke out over the issue of peaceful parliamentary transition to socialism. In an "Outline of Views on the Question of Peaceful Transition" submitted to the C.P.S.U. Central Committee, the Chinese maintained that it would be inadvisable to lay much stress on the possibility of peaceful transition, and especially on the possibility of seizing state power by winning a majority in parliament, for "it is liable to weaken the revolutionary will of the proletariat, the working people, and the communist party and disarm them ideologically." The Chinese document went on to express doubt whether there was a single country where the possibility of peaceful transition was of any practical significance. And, recalling Lenin's insistence that in a communist revolution the old state apparatus must be not simply taken over but destroyed, the Chinese warned that peaceful transition should not be interpreted in such a way as solely to mean transition through a parliamentary majority. That, the document concluded, would be a social democratic view, and: "On the question of socialist revolution, our position is fundamentally different from that of the social democratic parties. This distinction must not be obscured."[27]

Soviet sources have furnished no evidence to refute this account of the early development of the conflict that in our time has shaken and threatened to disrupt and even split in two the international communist movement. In the subsequent stages of the dispute, Chinese warnings against obscuring the distinction between the social democratic and communist positions on socialist revolution have given way to the charge that the Soviet leadership has gone the deradi-

---

27. *The Origin and Development of the Differences Between the Leadership of the C.P.S.U. and Ourselves* (Peking, 1963), pp. 11, 12, 59, 61. Soviet sources have asserted that the possibility of a parliamentary path of transition was mentioned in the 1952 new program of the British Communist party on Stalin's suggestion. It should be observed, however, that he did not make a corresponding general revision in *Soviet* Marxist doctrine.

calizing way of the social democratic leadership in Lenin's time. Khrushchevism has been seen as a new version of the Kautskyism that took over European Marxism a generation ago, and Lenin's writings of that time have been studied anew in search of insight into contemporary Soviet development. "As Lenin pointed out, the 'orthodox' Marxists headed by Kautsky were virtually hidden opportunists," declared a Chinese communist study of "Kautskyism" published in 1962:

> Under their leadership the Second International adopted some revolutionary manifestos and declarations, but their aim was not to put them into effect but to win the trust of the masses by fraud and to continue to manipulate the workers' movement.[28]

Four years later, all pretence of merely historical reference was thrown aside, and the Chinese communist leadership was saying:

> After Stalin's death, the leaders of the C.P.S.U. headed by Khrushchev gradually revealed their true features as betrayers of Lenin and Leninism and embarked on the old path of the German Social Democrats Bernstein and Kautsky, who betrayed Marx and Engels and Marxism.[29]

China and Deradicalization

Detailed treatment of the Sino-Soviet conflict is beyond the scope of the present study. The point I wish to make in

28. Li Fu, Li Ssu-Wen and Wang Fu-ju, "On Kautskyism," quoted in *Diversity in International Communism*, Alexander Dallin ed. (New York: Columbia University Press, 1963), pp. 277–278.

29. *Peking Review* 13 (March 25, 1966), p. 5.

conclusion is simply that in its inception, development, and basic content, this inner conflict in international communism shows a deeply significant similarity to (as well as significant differences from) the inner conflict that split the international social democratic Marxist movement after the First World War. Once again we see the leadership of some parts of the movement showing in their conduct and ideological pronouncements the symptoms of deradicalization. And once again we see rebellion against this trend on the part of radical elements of the movement in whom the need for integrity of theory and practice is still strong. Once again, moreover, the predominance of one element or the other is connected with the difference between the stages of development of the movement in one country and the other.

All this bears emphasizing in part because of a tendency of the Western mind to view the Sino-Soviet ideological controversy as a mere smokescreen for clashing national ambitions or great-power rivalry between Russia and China. To ignore the national, imperial, and personal factors in the conflict would be wrong. But it would be no less an error, and perhaps a greater one, to fail to perceive that ideological and political fundamentals of communism really are at stake in this dispute.

As recent events have clearly shown, moreover, the concern about Soviet deradicalization is accompanied in the mind of the Maoist leadership in China by a fear of deradicalizing tendencies in Chinese communism itself, and the conflict now in progress in the Chinese communist movement turns in large measure on this issue. To combat deradicalizing tendencies in the higher leadership as well as in the party and state apparatus throughout the country is an avowed main aim of the great Maoist "cultural revolution" that has convulsed the internal life of Communist China from 1966 to 1968. This aim—and in general the radical mentality—is epitomized in the slogan that has been given the youthful Maoist Red Guards: "Let us destroy the old world, and build a new world!" Mao and his closest adherents appear to realize more clearly than radical leaders of the past that the changing of the generations is always a threat to the radical mentality. "Imperialism pins its hopes of 'peaceful evolution' on the third and fourth generations," runs their reasoning as expressed in the Maoist press. "China's young people must remember class hatred and carry the proletarian revolutionary cause through to the end." To inoculate Communist China's young in advance against the bacilla of "revisionism" appears to be the purpose of the frenzied campaign of indoctrination. But it is not by indoctrination that genuine radical minds are created. The history of radical movements, Marxist ones included, suggests that Mao's fear of the coming deradicalization of Chinese communism is well founded.

Not often does a theoretical problem have such immediate relevance to the practical concerns of political leaders as in the present instance. Since statesmen in our time have had to deal with radical movements that have come to power and may have repeated occasion to do so in the future, an understanding of the dynamics of the behavior of such movements at various stages of their development is of great importance. Both the lack of such understanding and the need for it find illustration in the recent history of our thinking about Soviet communism. The Western mind has tended to anticipate a mellowing of the Soviet communist movement in terms of what has been called "ideological erosion." A decline or softening of official commitment to the final goals of the movement has, in other words, been taken as the prime criterion for judging whether Soviet communism is undergoing genuine change away from its radical foundations. The analysis presented in this study leads to a very different view. Not only would a Soviet communist movement in process of deradicalization go on proclaiming its adherence to the final goals of the movement; it would, by virtue of the dialectic of the process, reaffirm the goals in very strong terms, as it has done. For intensified *verbal* allegiance to ultimate ideological goals belongs to the pattern of deradicalization.

What a sociologist has written of religious change seems to be applicable also to ideological movements of radical persuasion: "Religious change is usually a latent process, carried on beneath symbols of nonchange."[30] Not the end of ideology but rather the growth of a stable discrepancy between ideological symbols and political deeds is the true mark of deradicalizing change in once-radical movements.

30. J. Milton Yinger, *Sociology Looks at Religion* (New York: Macmillan, 1963), p. 70. See also John H. Kautsky, "Myth, Self-Fulfilling Prophecy, and Symbolic Reassurance in the East-West Conflict," *Journal of Conflict Resolution*, 9 (March, 1965), pp. 11–12.

Chapter Seven

MARX AND THE
END OF HISTORY

◇◇◇◇◇◇◇◇◇◇◇◇◇◇◇◇◇◇◇◇◇◇◇◇◇◇◇◇

The hundred-and-fiftieth anniversary of Marx's birth is a more propitious occasion for commemoration of him than the hundredth would have been.[1] In May 1918, the world was at war, and not much concerned with such ceremonies. A party of Marxist revolutionaries had just taken power in Russia, but the future of that revolution, and others like it, was still unclear. And some early philosophical writings of Marx, knowledge of which was destined greatly to deepen our understanding of the genesis and meaning of Marxism, were still lying in archives and unknown to all but a very few. It was still too soon to assess the historical significance of Marx. Now we are better situated in time to make the assessment.

The most important of the early writings published since 1918 are the *Economic and Philosophical Manuscripts of*

1. An address presented at a symposium held in Trier on May 5, 1968, by the German UNESCO Commission to commemorate the hundred-and-fiftieth anniversary of Marx's birth.

1844. Here the young Marx set down a first systematic sketch of Marxism in concepts largely derived from post-Kantian German philosophy, Hegel's in particular. Deciphering what he conceived to be the "esoteric" meaning of Hegel's *Phenomenology of Mind*, he formulated his own conception of history as a process of self-development of the human species culminating in communism. Man, according to this conception, is essentially a producer; and material production is the primary form of his producing activity, industry being the externalized productive powers of the species. In the course of his history, which Marx described as a "history of production," a world of created objects gradually arises around man. Original nature is overlaid with a man-made "anthropological nature" or "nature produced by history." And Marx believed that this was the true or scientific restatement of the Hegelian conception. For had not Hegel seen the history of the world as a production-history on the part of the world-spirit? His error had been to mystify the process by treating the productive activity as *mental* activity primarily. To move from mystification to reality, from philosophy to science, one had only to turn Hegel on his head. Then it appeared that the Hegelian image of spirit creating a world was simply a philosopher's distorted picture of the reality of history, namely, that man—working man—creates a world in *material* productive activities over the centuries. Inevitably, therefore, Marx later named his transformed Hegelianism the "materialist conception of history."

Still following Hegel's basic scheme, Marx in the manuscripts visualized the human history of production as being also a history of estrangement (*Entfremdungsgeschichte*). Man's nature, he postulated, was to be a "free conscious producer," but so far he had not been able to express himself freely in productive activity. He had been driven to produce by need and greed, by a passion for accumulation which in the modern bourgeois age becomes accumulation of capital. His productive activity had always, therefore, been involuntary; it had been "labor." And since man, when he produces involuntarily, is estranged from his human nature, labor is "alienated labor." Escape from alienated labor finally becomes materially possible in the stage of technological development created by modern machine industry. The way of escape lies in the revolutionary seizure and socialization of the productive powers by the workers. Repossessed through revolution of his organs of material production externalized in industry, man will at last be able to produce in freedom. To Marx communism did not mean a new economic system. It meant the end of economics in a society where man, liberated from labor, would realize his creative nature in a life of leisure. So Marx defined communism in his manuscripts as "transcendence of human self-alienation," and saw it as the real future situation that Hegel had depicted in a mystified manner at the close of his *Phenomenology*, where spirit, having attained absolute knowledge, returns to itself out of its alienation and is fully "at home with itself in its otherness."

Such, very briefly, was Marxism as originally expounded; and it was this view of history that Marx and Engels elaborated in their voluminous later writings. Naturally, much was added and refined. Marx's thought, however, like that of most powerfully original thinkers, showed an underlying continuity. Indeed, *Capital*, published in 1867, was simply the form in which he finally finished and published the book he set out to write in his manuscripts of 1844.

Consequently, we are now able to see in him, far more clearly than anyone could easily have done a half-century ago, an heir and representative of the great age of German philosophy that started with Kant and ran its course through Schelling, Fichte, and Hegel to its diverse later outcomes. I do not mean to say that we should see him only as a philoso-

pher, or Marxism itself exclusively as a philosophical phenomenon. For Marx, as perhaps befitted a descendant of
rabbinical forbears, had a prophetic mission. The teaching
that he derived from philosophy and saw as science was
received widely as a new faith. It became the party ideology
of movements for revolution and, in our century, regimes of
revolution acting in Marx's name. Here, however, I am not
concerned with Marxism as a party ideology, but with Marx
as an intellectual and Marxism as *he* understood it. My question is this: What is his most important message to us now?
The answer I wish to suggest is that the aspect of Marx with
the greatest enduring significance and relevance for our
time is the utopian aspect, the part that we today might call
his "futurology." In order to explain this view, let me go a
few steps further in identifying his position.

If we ask ourselves what kind of philosopher Marx basically was, it is easy to answer that he was a philosopher of
history. For all his various attempts at a general definition
of his position were statements about the historical process.
Yet to describe Marx as a philosopher of history is to express
a rather superficial truth, because history per se was not the
primary object of his theorizing. The primary object was
man, man as a species and "species-being" (*Gattungswe-
sen*); and the theory of man is the matrix of Marx's theory
of history. He defines history as the *growth-process* of the
human species. In his own succinct statement in the 1844
manuscripts: "And just as all things natural must *become*,
man, too, has his act of becoming—*history*. . . .
Now this way of thinking carried the interesting implication that history has an end. Not in the sense of the world's
ending, for Marx assumed, in his pre-nuclear innocence, that
man and his world would exist indefinitely if not forever.
The end of history meant the end of the growth-process of

humanity, its emergence into adulthood. Although life and its vicissitudes would go on, and presumably some sorts of change would still occur, the historical agony of growing up, the long struggle of the species to *become* man—a class struggle in large part—would finally be over. The developmental stages of history, which Marx linked with successive "modes of production" from slave labor in antiquity through serf labor in the feudal period to wage labor in the bourgeois era, would be superseded by a radically new mode of productive activity and, along with it, an entirely new form of human community not subject to the dialectical dissolution and breakdown that had necessarily overtaken all historical forms of society. It was with this central idea in mind that Marx wrote in the preface to *The Critique of Political Economy* that the existing bourgeois social formation would bring to a close the prehistory of human society. It was another way of saying that the coming great revolution would usher in the post-historical phase of man's existence on this planet.

The notion of the adulthood of the species was meant by Marx with utmost philosophical seriousness. History as man's protracted "act of becoming" would give way in post-history to man's *being*, to his maturity on both a collective and individual scale. Only at the end could this occur, although the material conditions for it were developing all along. For alienation dogged humanity in every historical cycle of the growth-process, and indeed reached its lowest depth in the bourgeois era when man in the form of the wretched proletarian factory worker became a totally abased dehumanized being, an *Unmensch*. Thus, self-realization, or becoming fully human, was not for Marx a problem that an individual person could solve on his own. It could be solved only within the framework of the self-realization of the species at the end of history.

The normative concept of man implicit in this theory has already been touched upon. Man was seen as a spontaneously productive being with a need to express himself along a multitude of lines, and as tending in all his productive activities, material production included, to construct things "according to the laws of beauty." Marx's vision of the post-historical future was governed by this idea. Not only would machine industry be liberated to produce enough goods to meet the needs of all, but man himself would be liberated from the acquisitive drive, the obsession with wealth that had made him an alienated being. He would consequently be emancipated from the twin tyranny of need and specialization, from his age-old imprisonment in a life of labor and from the various enslaving forms of division of labor inherent in that life. The radically new mode of production coming in post-history would be the free creativity of individuals producing in cooperative association.

Marx not only conceived man as an artistic being in essence, but envisaged his post-historical relationship with "anthropological nature" in artistic terms. Unlike most modern Western philosophers, for whom the subject-object relation has presented primarily the problem of knowing, Marx hardly recognized this problem. Having translated Hegel materialistically, he saw the objects outside man as so many congealments of human productive activity combined with the stuff that the earth provided wherewith to make things. Consequently, their existence and knowability were not really in question. The posture of Cartesian doubt was not for Marx. How could it be for one whose imperative need was not to establish that a world exists but to explain why it appeared so unbearably ugly and oppressive —and to change it? Marx approached the problem of the subject-object relation from an aesthetic viewpoint.

The self-realization of the species would involve the humanization of the world that man had created, the "resurrection of nature." Having been produced in alienated labor and appropriated as private property, the world of objects made by human hand and machine confronted its makers during history as an "alienated world." The end of history would bring its de-alienation. After acquiring mastery of his productive powers and freedom to produce in a human way, man would refashion his own objectified nature according to the laws of beauty. Instead of confronting him as negations of himself, alien and hostile beings, the objects of his production would bring him self-confirmation. In addition to developing his productive talents in all directions, he would develop his capacity for aesthetic experience. His five senses would be cleansed gradually of the possessiveness, the "sense of having," that had always in the past defiled them and prevented him from perceiving and appreciating the intrinsic aesthetic quality of objects outside him. Consequently, reasoned Marx in his manuscripts of 1844, post-historical man would finally leave even communism behind. For communism, too, was a kind of ownership and possession—communal possession. With the complete humanization of man, even this form of possessiveness would be transcended. So we read in the manuscripts that "communism is the necessary form and energetic principle of the immediate future, but communism is not as such the goal of human development, the form of human society." Not communism as such but "positive humanism" was the goal of human development.

The idea of history having an end is not something new with Marx. In essence it as an eschatological idea with roots extending deep into the Judeo-Christian tradition. The heavenly afterlife was brought down to earth in the utopias of the Renaissance, the eighteenth-century Enlightenment, and the early nineteenth-century socialists. Marx built upon these foundations as well as upon German philosophy. But because of the Hegelian philosophical perspective from which he worked, and of the genius that he brought to the task, he created one of the most *relevant* of modern utopias.

What makes his futurology so pertinent to present problems is, I think, first of all the world scope of his conception of man's post-historical future. Marx was not a community-builder. He had no use for small-scale utopian community ventures carried out, as he once scornfully put it, "behind the back of society." That, to him, was utopianism in the pejorative sense. Being a philosopher of Hegelian formation, for whom history was meaningful only as world-history, he insisted from the start of his theorizing that the goal of human development could only be a new state of the world (*Weltzustand*). So he envisaged utopia on a global scale: man fully matured, master at last of his own powers and those of nature, exercising conscious control of the collective life-process, living the freely creative life in a universal human society.

Marx has been criticized for having little to say about community structures and institutional arrangements in post-historical society.[2] But such criticism may be misdirected in the final analysis, and in any event there is something to be said on the other side. A growing number of human problems have become or are fast becoming world problems, not resolvable within the confines of a single community or country or region, however large, although solutions may and should often *begin* locally. Not only war and arms-competition fall in this category, but also unchecked population growth, economic lag and food shortage, racialism, denial of human rights and freedoms, the squandering of mineral resources, the pollution of soil, water, and the earth's atmosphere, and so on. Progress can be made on such problems in nations and regions, but adequate solutions can-

2. For example, by Martin Buber, in *Paths in Utopia*, ch. 8, and in my *Philosophy and Myth in Karl Marx*, ch. 13.

not be found within any national or hemispheric or European or Atlantic or communist community but only within a universal human community. In our time, any serious utopia must be, like Marx's, a new state of the world.

His futurology also has relevance for us in its concrete envisagement of a future human life-style. Marx's concept of the "abolition of labor" in post-historical society anticipated certain present developments that are taking place owing to a technological revolution rather than the proletarian revolution forecast in the *Communist Manifesto*. Automation and the unlocking of the productive powers of the atom have begun to pose the question of a profound reorientation of man's existence, a reorientation from the work-centered life to a different kind of life. With the elimination of a great deal of economic labor, the problem of the *good* life may become inescapable for a growing proportion of mankind. What kind of living will then take the place of a large part of what has been called working for a living?

Marx's aesthetic utopia, his vision of a post-historical world where human existence takes on the character of creative leisure and artistic expression, represents at least one conceivable answer. Since men in the mass may not have as much artistic bent as he imputed to human nature and may not regard leisure as the unmitigated blessing he thought it would be, we cannot take his utopia as a statement of the inevitable. It still has value, however, as a preview of what is possible. And his notion of the entire environment as a field for aesthetic effort, of "anthropological nature" itself as man's supreme work of art, is particularly pertinent in an age that has seen so much spoliation of nature, destruction of natural beauty, and spread of urban blight. Who in our time, living in big cities, can doubt the imperative need for what Marx called the "true resurrection of nature"?

There is possible guidance for us, finally, in his fundamental concept of the growing up of the race, the graduation of man from his historical growth-process into adulthood. Not that we can take a happy ending of history for granted any longer. Living in the final third of the twentieth century, with great tragedies behind and dangers ahead, we cannot anticipate the future in a Marxian spirit of millenarian optimism. We can see that man may not achieve a universal community, that he may not gain mastery of his powers, that the world's population may go on exploding, that racialism and nationalism may continue to flourish, that life may grow poorer in an increasingly crowded, impersonal, coercive, and regimented society, and that—in the warning words of Erik H. Erikson—"Reactionary rage equipped with atomic weapons may mean the end of man just when for the first time he has a chance to become one species."[3] But the very hugeness of these dangers suggests that *without* some such breakthrough to human maturity as Marx was talking about, the cause may be lost. What I mean to say is that the least likely future may be one in which man muddles through more or less as he has been doing, governments show no more imagination and moral leadership than they have been showing, and history goes on as usual.

The precondition of successful human adaptation and even survival may be radical change—not so much in the organizational arrangements for living as in the consciousness of people, their attitudes to others and themselves, their sense of responsibility to distant peoples and future generations, their patterns of feeling and identity. This is to say that further growth is essential, that the species may now be in a "maturation crisis." If so, one of the most serious aspects of the crisis is the general lack of awareness of

3. R. I. Evans, *Dialogue with Erik Erikson* (New York, Evanston, and London: Harper and Row, 1967), p. 33.

it, the tendency of most people and even the leaders of nations to assume that no great change is called for, that no enlargement of the human spirit is necessary, that we immature humans are already grown up. Marx therefore may be at his most relevant in telling us that this is not so, that the species is still engaged in its historical act of becoming and has not yet fully achieved the condition of *being* human.

It must be said, in conclusion, that he was far more effective in grasping these fundamentals and envisaging a fully human future than he was in specifying the means of bringing it about. He greatly overestimated material and technological development as the prerequisite of human maturation, failing to see the immense psychological difficulties and the consequent critical role of leadership and education in the process. He imagined, mistakenly, that revolutionary force and violence could be the means of achieving not only a new society but the new adult human being as its inhabitant; and so he left to such teachers as Gandhi and Martin Luther King, Jr., the task of showing men how to change society, nonviolently, by changing themselves. Finally, and as a result, Marx thought that the revolutionary process of man's maturation could take place very rapidly once the conditions were ripe. He did not understand that the growing up of collective man is bound to be—like the growing up of individuals—a protracted process marked by partial advances, occasional breakthroughs, inevitable setbacks, and only eventual success.

But he was not the first prophet to be more successful in pointing out the promised land than in leading people to it. His genius lay in his powers of visualizing the end. In an age when utopianism has become the only realism, these powers are needed as never before.

Bibliographic Note

The very large literature on Marx and Marxism has been growing with unprecedented rapidity in the past decade. Thus, a recent bibliography of only one important sphere of Marx studies (John Lachs, *Marxist Philosophy: A Bibliographical Guide*, 1967) comes to over one hundred fifty pages. The titles listed below, besides being confined to books in English, constitute no more than a small personal selection of studies that may be useful for further reading on themes of the present volume.

The Marxist Writings

The most useful collection is the two-volume Marx and Engels, *Selected Works* (Moscow: Foreign Languages Publishing House, several editions), now available in a single paperbound volume under the same title (New York: International Publishers, 1968). Two single-volume selections of note are Karl Marx and Friedrich Engels, *Basic Writings on Politics and Philosophy**, ed. Lewis S. Feuer (Garden City: Doubleday Anchor, 1959) and Arthur P. Mendel, ed., *Essential Works of Marxism** (New York: Bantam Books, 1961). For Marx's early writings, including the *Economic and Philosophical Manuscripts of 1844*, T. B. Bottomore, ed., *Karl Marx, Early Writings** (New York: McGraw-Hill, 1964).

The writings of social democratic Marxism include: Karl Kautsky, *The Class Struggle (Erfurt Program)* (Chicago: Charles H. Kerr, 1910); Karl Kautsky, *The Social Revolution* (Chicago: Charles H. Kerr, 1913); Karl Kautsky, *The Dictatorship of the Proletariat** (Ann Arbor: The University of Michigan Press, 1964); G. Plekhanov, *Socialism and the Political Struggle*, in *Selected Philosophical Works* (Moscow: Foreign Languages Publishing House); and Julius Martov, *The State and the Socialist Revolution* (New

* indicates paperbound edition

York, 1939). For the revisionist position, the chief statement is Eduard Bernstein, *Evolutionary Socialism: A Criticism and Affirmation** (New York: Schocken Books, 1961).

The foundations of communist Marxism were laid by Lenin in the major writings gathered in the three-volume V. I. Lenin, *Selected Works** (New York: International Publishers, 1968). A useful single-volume anthology is James Connor, ed., *Lenin on Politics and Revolution* (New York: Pegasus, 1968). Stalin's principal theoretical work, *The Foundations of Leninism*, is included in Mendel, *The Essential Works of Marxism**, as is the 1961 C.P.S.U. Party Program. For Bukharin's contribution, before he became the main theorist of the right-wing position, see N. Bukharin and E. Preobrazhensky, *The ABC of Communism** (Ann Arbor: The University of Michigan Press, 1966) and Nikolai Bukharin, *Historical Materialism: A System of Sociology* (New York: International Publishers, 1925). For Trotsky's contributions to communist Marxism, see especially *Permanent Revolution and Results and Prospects** (New York: Pioneer Publications, 1962); *The New Course** (Ann Arbor: The University of Michigan Press, 1965); *Terrorism and Communism** (Ann Arbor: The University of Michigan Press, 1961); and *The Revolution Betrayed** (New York: Merit Publications, 1937). O. V. Kuusinen, chief ed., *Fundamentals of Marxism-Leninism* (Moscow: Foreign Languages Publishing House, 1961) is a manual of Soviet Marxism of the post-Stalinist period. For the major theoretical writings of Mao, see Mao Tse-tung, *Selected Works* in four volumes (New York: International Publishers, 1954–1956). For Yugoslav Marxist doctrine: Edvard Kardelj, *Socialism and War* (London: Methuen, 1961) and V. Benes, R. Byrnes, and N. Spulber, eds., *The Second Soviet-Yugoslav Dispute* (Bloomington: Indiana University Publications).

The translated writings of the critical humanist Marxists of the communist world include: L. Kolakowsky, *Toward a Marxist Humanism* (New York: Grove Press, 1968); L. Kolakowsky, *The Alienation of Reason* (Garden City: Doubleday, 1968); Gajo Petrovic, *Marx in the Mid-Twentieth Century: A Yugoslav Philosopher Reconsiders Karl Marx's Writings** (Garden City: Doubleday Anchor, 1967); and various essays in Erich Fromm, ed., *Socialist Humanism: An International Symposium** (Garden City: Doubleday Anchor, 1965). See also articles in the international edition of the journal *Praxis*, published in Zagreb.

Surveys

On the background and development of classical Marxism: G. D. H. Cole, *Socialist Thought: The Forerunners 1789–1850* and *Socialist Thought: Marxism and Anarchism 1850–1890* (London: Macmillan, St. Martin's Press, 1953–1954); George Lichtheim, *Marxism: An Historical and Critical Survey** (New York: Praeger, 1961); Herbert Marcuse, *Reason and Revolution: Hegel and the Rise of Social Theory* (Boston: The Beacon Press, 1954); Adam Ulam, *The Unfinished Revolution: An Essay on the Sources of Influence of Marxism and Communism** (New York: Random House, 1960); Bertram D. Wolfe, *Marxism: One Hundred Years in the Life of a Doctrine** (New York: Dell Publishing Co., 1965); and Robert C. Tucker, *Philosophy and Myth in Karl Marx** (Cambridge: The Cambridge University Press, 1961).

On the development of social democratic Marxism: James Joll, *The Second International 1889–1914** (New York: Harper & Row, 1955); George Lichtheim, *Marxism;* Alfred G. Meyer, *Marxism: The Unity of Theory and Practice** (Ann Arbor: The University of Michigan Press, 1963); Peter Gay, *The Dilemma of Democratic Socialism: Eduard Bernstein's Challenge to Marx** (New York: Collier Macmillan Co., 1952); and J. P. Nettl, *Rosa Luxemburg*, two volumes (Oxford University Press, 1966).

On the development of communist Marxism: Nicholas Berdyaev, *The Origin of Russian Communism** (Ann Arbor: The University of Michigan Press, 1955); F. Dan, *The Origins of Bolshevism.* trans. Joel Carmichael (New York: Harper & Row, 1964); Leopold Haimson, *The Russian Marxists and the Origins of Bolshevism** (Boston: The Beacon Press, 1955); Arthur Mendel, *Dilemmas of Progress in Tsarist Russia: Legal Marxism and Legal Populism* (Cambridge, Mass.: Harvard University Press, 1961); Herbert Marcuse, *Soviet Marxism: A Critical Analysis* (New York: Columbia University Press, 1958); Richard T. De George, *Patterns of Soviet Thought: Origins and Development of Dialectical and Historical Materialism* (Ann Arbor: The University of Michigan Press, 1966), and *The New Marxism: Soviet and East European Marxism Since 1956** (New York: Pegasus, 1968); and Benjamin I. Schwartz, *Chinese Communism and the Rise of Mao** (New York: Harper & Row, 1961).

On the Early Marx and Alienation

The *Economic and Philosophical Manuscripts of 1844* (in *Early Writings**, mentioned above) and other writings of the young Karl Marx were first published earlier in the present century, revealing an "original Marxism" which expounded the materialist conception of history in terms of man's "alienation" and the overcoming of alienation through a communist revolution. These writings implicitly raised a number of basic questions about the genesis and meaning of Marxism: What was Marxism's relation to foregoing German philosophy, Hegel's and Feuerbach's in particular? What was the relation between the "young" and the "old" Marx? Was the alienation theme something of importance in Marxism or merely a terminological device sloughed off by the time of the *Communist Manifesto?* Did the later Marxist writings, above all *Capital,* show the continuing influence of the concept of man's alienation upon the mind of Marx? Inevitably, a scholarly controversy developed around these questions.

For the older viewpoint that attached little if any importance to the 1844 manuscripts and the alienation theme in Marxism, see particularly Sidney Hook, *From Hegel to Marx: Studies in the Intellectual Development of Karl Marx* (Ann Arbor: University of Michigan Press, 1950), and especially the second edition* (Ann Arbor: The University of Michigan Press, 1962), which has a new introduction dealing directly with the alienation issue. For the position that Marx's Marxism is fundamentally about alienation and that there is in this respect a basic continuity of thought from the 1844 manuscripts to *Capital,* despite changes in terminology, see Robert C. Tucker, *Philosophy and Myth in Karl Marx**. The continuity theme has been stressed in S. Avineri, *The Social and Political Thought of Karl Marx* (Cambridge: The Cambridge University Press, 1968), as well as in Raya Dunaevskaya, *Marxism and Freedom* (New York: Bookman Associates, 1958), Erich Fromm's introduction to E. Fromm, ed., *Marx's Concept of Man** (New York: Frederick Ungar, 1961), and other studies. On the early Marx see also Eugene Kamenka, *The Ethical Foundations of Marxism* (London: Routledge, 1962); Gajo Petrovic, *Marx in the Mid-Twentieth Century** (Doubleday Anchor); and various essays in E. Fromm, ed., *Socialist Humanism.* On Marx in relation to the existentialists, see Walter Odajynk, *Marxism and Existentialism* (Garden City: Doubleday Anchor, 1965).

On Marxist Social and Political Theory

Among the significant works of critical exposition and interpretation are: M. M. Bober, *Karl Marx's Interpretation of History** (New York: W. W. Norton, 1950); Karl Federn, *The Materialist Conception of History: A Critical Analysis** (New York: International Publishers, 1939); Ralf Dahrendorf, *Class and Class Conflict in Industrial Society** (Stanford: Stanford University Press, 1959); John Plamenatz, *Man and Society*, II (New York: McGraw-Hill, 1963); Martin Buber, *Paths in Utopia** (The Beacon Press, 1949); and the introduction to T. B. Bottomore and Maximilien Rubel, eds., Karl Marx, *Selected Writings in Sociology and Social Philosophy** (New York: McGraw-Hill Book Co). For the relation between Marxism and the Anarchist political doctrines, see especially James Joll, *The Anarchists* (Boston and Toronto: Little, Brown and Company, 1964).

Marxism and Modernization

There is very little literature specifically dealing with Marxism as a theory of modernization, but quite a few studies are directly or indirectly related to this problem. See in particular: Adam Ulam, *The Unfinished Revolution** (New York: Random House); W. W. Rostow, *The Stages of Economic Growth** (Cambridge: Cambridge University Press, 1960); Karl Polanyi, *The Great Transformation** (Boston: The Beacon Press, 1944); Alexander Gerschenkron, *Economic Backwardness in Historical Perspective** (New York: Praeger, 1965); E. Preobrazhensky, *The New Economics*, trans. Brian Pearce (Oxford: Clarendon Press, 1965); Arthur P. Mendel, *Dilemmas of Progress in Tsarist Russia;* Herbert Marcuse, *Soviet Marxism;* Alexander Erlich, *The Soviet Industrialization Debate, 1924–1928* (Cambridge, Mass.: Harvard University Press, 1950);

Barrington Moore, *Soviet Politics—The Dilemma of Power: The Role of Ideas in Social Change** (New York: Harper and Row, 1950); and Alfred G. Meyer, *Leninism** (New York: Praeger, 1957).

On Deradicalization

Some of the principal relevant writings are: Robert Michels, *Political Parties** (New York: Dover Publications, 1959); L. Trotsky, *The New Course** and *The Revolution Betrayed**; James Joll, *The Second International 1889–1914*; Alfred G. Meyer, *Marxism: The Unity of Theory and Practice* (Ann Arbor: The University of Michigan Press, 1953); Peter Gay, *The Dilemma of Democratic Socialism**; Robert V. Daniels, *The Conscience of the Revolution: Communist Opposition in Soviet Russia* (Cambridge, Mass.: Harvard University Press, 1960); Isaac Deutscher, *The Prophet Unarmed. Trotsky: 1921–1929* (New York: Vintage Books, 1965); and Barrington Moore, *Soviet Politics—The Dilemma of Power**.

Index

Publications of the
Center of International Studies
Princeton University

Almond, Gabriel A., *The Appeals of Communism* (Princeton University Press, 1954), $7.50 (cloth); $2.95 (paper).

Kaufmann, William W., ed., *Military Policy and National Security* (Princeton University Press, 1956), $5.00.

Knorr, Klaus, *The War Potential of Nations* (Princeton University Press, 1956), $6.50.

Pye, Lucian W., *Guerrilla Communism in Malaya* (Princeton University Press, 1956), $6.95.

De Visscher, Charles, trans. by P. E. Corbett, *Theory and Reality in Public International Law* (Princeton University Press, 1957, rev. ed. 1968), $12.50.

Cohen, Bernard C., *The Political Process and Foreign Policy: The Making of the Japanese Peace Settlement* (Princeton University Press, 1957), $6.00.

Weiner, Myron, *Party Politics in India: The Development of a Multi-Party System* (Princeton University Press, 1957), $6.00.

Corbett, Percy E., *Law in Diplomacy* (Princeton University Press, 1959), out of print.

Sannwald, Rolf and Jacques Stohler, trans. by Herman Karreman, foreword by Klaus Knorr, *Economic Integration: Theoretical Assumptions and Consequences of European Integration* (Princeton University Press, 1959), out of print.

Knorr, Klaus, ed., *NATO and American Security* (Princeton University Press, 1959), $7.50.

Almond, Gabriel A. and James Coleman, eds., *The Politics of the Developing Areas* (Princeton University Press, 1960), $8.50.

Kahn, Herman, *On Thermonuclear War* (Princeton University Press, 1960), $12.50.

Verba, Sidney, *Small Groups and Political Behavior: A Study of Leadership* (Princeton University Press, 1961), $6.00.

Butow, Robert J. C., *Tojo and the Coming of the War* (Princeton University Press, 1961), $10.00.

Snyder, Glenn II., *Deterrence and Defense: Toward a Theory of National Security* (Princeton University Press, 1961), $6.50.

Knorr, Klaus and Sidney Verba, eds., *The International System: Theoretical Essays* (Princeton University Press, 1961), $5.00 (cloth); $2.95 (paper).

Paret, Peter and John W. Shy, *Guerrillas in the 1960's* (Frederick A. Praeger, Inc., 1962), $3.50.

Modelski, George, *A Theory of Foreign Policy* (Frederick A. Praeger, Inc., 1962), $5.00.

Knorr, Klaus and Thornton Read, eds., *Limited Strategic War* (Frederick A. Praeger, Inc., 1962), $6.00.

Dunn, Frederick S., *Peace-Making and the Settlement with Japan* (Princeton University Press, 1963), $5.00.

Burns, Arthur L. and Nina Heathcote, *Peace-Keeping by United Nations Forces: From Suez Through the Congo* (Frederick A. Praeger, Inc., 1963), $6.00.

Falk, Richard A., *Law, Morality and War in the Contemporary World* (Frederick A. Praeger, Inc., 1963), $4.00.

Rosenau, James N., National *Leadership and Foreign Policy: A Case Study in the Mobilization of Public Support* (Princeton University Press, 1963), $8.50.

Almond, Gabriel A. and Sidney Verba, *The Civic Culture: Political Attitudes and Democracy in Five Nations* (Princeton University Press, 1963), $8.50.

Cohen, Bernard C., *The Press and Foreign Policy* (Princeton University Press, 1963), $6.00 (cloth); $2.95 (paper).

Sklar, Richard L., *Nigerian Political Parties: Power in an Emergent African Nation* (Princeton University Press, 1963), $12.50.

Paret, Peter, *French Revolutionary Warfare from Indochina to Algeria: The Analysis of a Political and Military Doctrine* (Frederick A. Praeger, Inc., 1964), $4.95.

Eckstein, Harry, ed., *Internal War* (Free Press, 1964), $6.50.

Black, Cyril E. and Thomas P. Thornton, eds., *Communism and Revolution: The Strategic Uses of Political Violence* (Princeton University Press, 1964), $10.00 (cloth); $2.95 (paper).

Camps, Miriam, *Britain and the European Community 1955–1963* (Princeton University Press, 1964), $8.50.

Thornton, Thomas P., ed., *The Third World in Soviet Perspective: Studies by Soviet Writers on the Developing Areas* (Princeton University Press, 1964), $7.50.

Rosenau, James N., ed., *International Aspects of Civil Strife* (Princeton University Press, 1964), $7.50.

Ploss, Sidney L., *Conflict and Decision-Making in Soviet Russia: A Case Study of Agricultural Policy, 1953–1963* (Princeton University Press, 1965), $6.50 (cloth); $2.95 (paper).

Falk, Richard A. and Richard J. Barnet, eds., *Security in Disarmament* (Princeton University Press, 1965), $10.00 (cloth); $2.95 (paper).

Von Vorys, Karl, *Political Development in Pakistan* (Princeton University Press, 1965), $6.50.

Sprout, Harold and Margaret, *The Ecological Perspective on Human Affairs* (Princeton University Press, 1965), $5.50.

Knorr, Klaus, *On the Uses of Military Power in the Nuclear Age* (Princeton University Press, 1966), $5.00.

Eckstein, Harry, *Division and Cohesion in Democracy, A Study of Norway* (Princeton University Press, 1966), $6.75.

Black, Cyril E., *The Dynamics of Modernization: A Study in Conparative History* (Harper and Row, 1966), $5.95.

Kunstadter, Peter, ed., *Southeast Asian Tribes, Minorities and Nations* (Princeton University Press, 1967), 2 vols., $28.50.

Wolfenstein, E. Victor, *The Revolutionary Personality: Lenin, Trotsky, Gandhi* (Princeton University Press, 1967), $7.50.

Young, Oran R., *The Intermediaries: Third Parties in International Crises* (Princeton University Press, 1967), $10.00.

Rosenau, James N., ed., *Domestic Sources of Foreign Policy* (Free Press, 1967), $7.50.

Hamilton, Richard F., *Affluence and the French Worker in the Fourth Republic* (Princeton University Press, 1967), $8.50.

Miller, Linda B., *World Order and Local Disorder: The United Nations and Internal Conflicts* (Princeton University Press, 1967), $6.50.

Bienen, Henry, *Tanzania: Party Transformation and Economic Development* (Princeton University Press, 1967), $11.50.

Ullman, Richard H., *Britain and the Russian Civil War: November 1918–February 1920*. Volume II of *Anglo-Soviet Relations, 1917–1921* (Princeton University Press, 1968), $10.00.

Gilpin, Robert, *France in the Age of the Scientific State* (Princeton University Press, 1968), $12.50.

Bader, William B., *The United States and the Spread of Nuclear Weapons* (Pegasus, 1968), $6.00.

Falk, Richard A., *Legal Order in a Violent World* (Princeton University Press, 1968), $15.00.

PUBLICATIONS

Black, Cyril E., Richard A. Falk, Klaus Knorr, and Oran R. Young, *Neutralization and World Politics* (Princeton University Press, 1968), $7.50 (cloth); $1.95 (paper).

Young, Oran R., *The Politics of Force* (Princeton University Press), 1969.

Knorr, Klaus and James N. Rosenau, eds., *Contending Approaches to International Politics* (Princeton University Press, 1969).

Rosenau, James N., ed., *Linkage Politics: Essays on the Convergence of National and International Systems* (Free Press, 1969).

Falk, Richard A., *The Status of Law in International Society* (Princeton University Press, 1969).

Falk, Richard A. and Cyril E. Black, eds., *The Future of the International Legal Order*. Vol. I, *Trends and Patterns* (Princeton University Press, 1969).

Falk, Richard A. and Cyril E. Black, eds., *The Future of the International Legal Order*. Vol. II, *Wealth and Resources* (Princeton University Press, 1969).